My illness and the sudden withdrawal of ACTH caused my weight to drop from a bloated 200 pounds to a skinny 120; wrinkled, jaundiced skin draped my bones. I was uncomfortable and miserable, and most routine hospital procedures were impossible for me. I felt like a codfish being thrown on a slab when the orderlies plopped me on a board to weigh me. My dignity was gone, and I felt like so much garbage. It didn't seem possible that I'd ever be normal again. The doctors and nurses had just about given up. Then. . . .

·HOW·GREAT· ·I·WAS·!

by DOUG FOLEY

Whitaker House

© 1974 by Whitaker House
Printed in the United States of America
International Standard Book Number
0-88368-041-6

All rights reserved. No portion of this book may be used in any form without the written permission of the publisher, with exception of brief excerpts in magazine articles, reviews, etc.

Whitaker House
504 Laurel Drive
Monroeville, Pennsylvania 15146

Some of the names in this book have been changed to protect the individuals involved. The events are absolutely as described.

To Barbara Carol, my wife, who brings me joy and encouragement. Without her assistance this book would be only a dream.

CONTENTS

Introduction ix

ONE: *By What Bootstraps?* 1
TWO: *Dented Pride* 7
THREE: *City Slickers 'n' Country Folks* 15
FOUR: *Playing Second Fiddle to Jesus* 21
FIVE: *From 200 Pounds to 120* 33
SIX: *Every Good Garden Needs Fertilizer* 43
SEVEN: *The Pot and the Potter* 55
EIGHT: *Sackcloth and Ashes* 67
NINE: *No Silver-tongued Orator* 79
TEN: *Hums, Buzzes and Uh-ohs* 87
ELEVEN: *The Bleating of Sheep* 97
TWELVE: *Every Rung Goes Higher, Higher* 105

Epilogue 113

INTRODUCTION

When the twelve-year-old Doug Foley looked angelic in his white robe, serving as acolyte in his parents' church, Gertrude Warner, authoress of such wonderful children's books as *The Box Car Children*, collared him one day and told him that God had a calling on his life.

After many years and many struggles, this calling has been realized. When Miss Warner heard about Doug's ministry, she wrote him a delightful letter. In it she expressed how very happy she was that Doug was not the kind of minister who "put on ham and bean suppers on Saturday nights in order to raise money to buy lace doilies for ladies' luncheons!"

I'll have to vouch for that. Doug is certainly not that kind of preacher. He's not satisfied unless he is moving in the power of the Holy Spirit, seeing God change lives and heal sick bodies. But there is a price for such a ministry.

Though the beginning of Doug's Christian experience was marked by the pride of life, God knew exactly how to remake him into a usable vessel. This is the story of Doug's personal struggles with an "incurable" disease, which God allowed to batter him in a divine crucible until He was ready for the Master's use. When I read parts of this story, I can't help wiping away a few tears at the memories. As husband and wife, Doug and I have shared many hard struggles. But today I can rejoice as we experience the joy of serving a most real, loving, and powerful God.

Barbara Carol Foley

Chapter One

BY WHAT BOOTSTRAPS?

I hope you have read in My Word that "pride goeth before destruction, and an haughty spirit before a fall." * That is far more than a statement of fact; that is a foretelling of things to come. For where there is haughtiness and self-sufficiency, you may be sure that I, the Lord, will permit stumbling and falling and breaking of spirit.

"Oh God, what did I do wrong? God, why? Why me?" I whimpered more to myself than to God or anyone else. I cowered in the corner of the four-bed ward with the curtains pulled around my bed.

The men in the other three beds were the "usual" sick, I assumed, since they didn't seem particularly

---
* Proverbs 16:18.

scared. Broken bones or an operation was no doubt the worst of their troubles. They'd get over their problem in a few days, or a few months at most. But not me. I was doomed.

I could hear people scurrying around. Over the PA system came frequent messages that Dr. So-and-So or Dr. Such-and-Such should report here or there. A medicinal odor filled the air. The Hartford hospital was hectic and understaffed, as most hospitals are today. Little emergencies cropped up repeatedly—as, for instance, when a young visitor walked into my room and collapsed about a foot from the door at the sight of his friend, Bobby, who lay in the bed across from me. Bobby had been pretty well banged up in an auto accident. Hospitals made my stomach queasy too, but like it or not, I'd be in one for a while.

An aide had just helped me back into bed after my visit with the neurologist who had been elected to break the news to me. In a small hospital office used for consultations, the neurologist had stumbled all over himself in an effort to find words that would soften the blow. I could tell he was finding it very difficult to keep his voice controlled while giving me, a very young man at the threshold of life, the news that my life was shattered. I would never be normal. (These are the times, I'm sure, when doctors must wish they had picked another profession.)

"What's wrong with me?" I had asked fearfully.

"Disseminated sclerosis."

That didn't *sound* quite as dreadful as "multiple sclerosis," but I knew it meant the same. I'd never known such emptiness. I felt as if I'd begun a walk down death row.

In time I would come to understand how the myelin sheath (nerve covering) would be eaten away as the disease progressed. Then, with the covering eaten away, nerve impulses would be "short-circuited" and I would loose sensory and/or motor control, depending on which bundle of nerves was attacked. I would experience the fear of going to sleep lest I find more damage when I awoke. I would come to know the nightmarish horror of immobility and numbness, and the havoc they play with the mind as well as the body. I'd know the fear of wondering how long the attacks would last and how much of me would be left usable when they were over. I would experience, too, mental anguish accompanying each adjustment to added handicaps.

For the moment, however, I didn't clearly understand. All I knew was that within the ten-day period before my consultation with the neurologist I had become blind. And nobody was assuring me that my situation would improve. I wasn't aware that other parts of my body could be hit at any time. But the doctor knew, and he was endeavoring to put a splint on my mental backbone, so that I wouldn't crack completely under more of these hideous assaults on my body.

At the age of twenty-four, I was as good as dead. My engineering career had gone down the drain. All my education was wasted. My dreams were foolishness. I didn't understand all the implications at that moment, but I did know my life would never again be as it had been. What would I do? What about my wife? A family? The basic enjoyments in life?

I knew my wife loved me—but how could I expect, or even allow her to stay with me? Sure, we'd said, "for better or for worse"—but neither of us had bargained for a "worse" this bad! If the shoe were on the other foot, I knew I'd be tempted to skip; I didn't consider myself any martyr. How could I expect Barbara to be one?

Our first wedding anniversary came while I was in the hospital. Needless to say, celebrating it was the farthest thing from our minds. But Barbara was with me, and that was all that was important. She assured me that she had every intention of sticking by me, even if it did mean "for worse." She became my security blanket. Whenever she was around I felt safe and secure, like a child feels when he's with his mother. All self-sufficiency had disappeared.

Barbara couldn't be with me all the time, however. Someone had to support us. So while she worked, I spent long, lonely days in the hospital with plenty of time to contemplate the future. In those hours, I would reflect on her encouraging words; but then I would think maybe that's all they were—just words. Maybe she didn't really mean it when she said she'd stick by me. So I spent most of the time having a real pity-party for myself. But eventually even the tears dried up, and emptiness and helplessness gnawed at the pit of my stomach.

A fellow named Pete was in the bed next to mine. I'd think how lucky he was. He had a broken leg, and

I figured he'd get better. But somehow I knew I wouldn't.

And then there was Bob. His mother sickened me by the way she doted over her "poor Bobby" when she came to visit. He'd totaled his car after a drunken binge, and I thought he deserved what he got.

Everyone and everything around me were annoyances. I was void of compassion for my fellow sufferers. I felt I'd been dealt a dirty deal in life, and all I wanted to do was crawl into a hole, curl up, and die. The emotions I lived with were bitterness, depression, and fear. The doctor's only advice was, "Now, son, you'll just have to pull yourself up by the bootstraps and live with it."

"Big deal," I said under my breath. "My boots don't *have* any straps."

One morning Pete started telling me about himself, just to make conversation and pass the time of day. Why he picked on me, I didn't understand. I was certainly not pleasant company. Pete was a teamster who had landed in the hospital after falling off the back end of a truck and breaking his leg. The accident happened there in Hartford, which was a two-hour drive from Pete's home. He had few visitors, since his family and friends were so far away.

I knew that Pete wasn't as well off as I'd assumed. The injury had stirred up an old ailment in his leg— osteomyelitis. Because of this, the doctors had put him in traction and told him he'd have to stay in Hartford; his condition made it unsafe to move him to a hospital nearer his home.

During our talk that morning, Pete told me that he

had an experience with God and now knew Him as a reality. He also told me about the church he belonged to, and how they prayed for the sick there. Healings had taken place as a result of prayer, he assured me. He was believing God for his own healing; if God *didn't* do something, there was a chance his leg would be amputated.

I listened. Pete wasn't a kook. He was about my age and seemed to have a good head on his shoulders. But we didn't talk long; I was too bound up in self-pity to respond to him. I rolled over and turned on the radio.

"The Hour of Decision is brought to you by the Billy Graham Evangelistic Association," the announcer said.

I'd been to a Billy Graham crusade when I was fifteen years old. I was impressionable then and had gone forward when the invitation was given. It was a pleasant experience and, for a short while following the crusade, I toyed with the idea of becoming a preacher. I quickly learned, however, that preachers just don't make enough of that "green stuff," so I gave up that notion, and went back to life as it had been previously.

I usually turned off religious broadcasts, but I heard this one out. It struck me as odd that Dr. Graham repeatedly used a phrase I had just heard from Pete: "born again." I wasn't sure what that meant, but I was impressed by the coincidence.

"Maybe I ought to try God," I thought. *"What can I lose?"*

Chapter Two

DENTED PRIDE

Did I not say, "The pride of thine heart hath deceived thee"? [*] *You thought you were sufficient unto yourself. You thought you were strong and able to cope with any problem that might arise. But when I withdrew My protecting hand from you, what were you then?*

Barbara took care of the hospital discharge details. Before I got out the door, Pete reminded me about our conversation. He encouraged me to check out what he'd said and maybe visit his church.

I was then wheeled out of my room after about six weeks of hospital confinement, and an orderly helped me into the car. The doctors were allowing me to go

---
[*] Obadiah 3.

home because medical science had done all it could for me—nothing.

Barbara drove us to my parents' home in Putnam, where we'd planned to stay until "whatever" happened.

I could think of only one thing to be thankful for: Two weeks before blindness had socked me, I had traded my Chevy Super Sport convertible for a more family-type car. If I'd kept it, we'd have been without transportation, since Barbara couldn't drive it. The Super Sport, with its heavy-duty truck clutch, four-speed transmission, and 409-cubic-inch engine, was my special baby. I felt like a real big shot when I revved up the noisy tank. My "good" reason for trading was that Barbara couldn't push the clutch down even with two feet; my *real* reason may have had something to do with the fact that *I* found it almost impossible to drive the thing in city traffic.

I couldn't get used to living in darkness and needing help to do even the simplest things, like putting toothpaste on my toothbrush and finding the right pair of socks. Mom gave us my old room, and watched out for me while Barbara went to work every day. I'll never know how she put up with my demands on her time. For hours each day I would have her drive me all over the countryside, describing to me the colors of the fall foliage. Riding was my favorite pastime. It eased my mind until my wife came in from the office around six.

Traditionally it's the wife who waits home for the husband to return from the office, and *a warped situation like ours put a big dent in my pride. I had a certain "thing"* about being the provider, the strong one. Pride filled every part of my life—as it seems to with many men—in subtle ways and in not-so-subtle ways.

My family tried to do everything to make me happy, but it seemed impossible for me to adjust. Mealtimes were horrible. Sometimes I couldn't find the food on my plate, or I'd drop a forkful of mashed potatoes in my lap.

One time my younger brother, who was totally sympathetic toward me, became so upset while watching me eat that his emotions got the best of him and he gave way to a nervous giggle. That's all I needed—to hear someone laughing at me! Angry and embarrassed, I tore out of the kitchen, leaving everyone else feeling guilty and sick over their inability to help me.

In my despair, I began to think about what Pete had told me in the hospital. Maybe God had an answer for my dilemma. So every night after supper I'd have Barbara read the Bible to me.

We started in the book of Matthew and began to go right through the New Testament. Neither one of us got a whole lot out of it at first, but the Bible was the only place where I thought perhaps I might find some sort of key for my healing. I was determined we'd drudge our way through it.

I was alone one day while Barbara was working and Mom was ironing. Mom had finally convinced me that occasionally she had to do something more than ride around. I still hadn't adjusted enough to my dark world to do anything useful, so I'd pace around from room to room, making a big circle through the house.

Tired of feeling my way, I sat down on the living-room couch. Barbara and I had been reading and studying the Bible together for several weeks now, and I was finding that some of it was pretty interesting. It seemed good to be occupied with something other than fear for a moment. One Scripture seemed to stick out to me more than the rest. It said, "All things, whatsoever ye shall ask in prayer, believing, ye shall receive" (Matthew 21:22). I mulled that over for a while. Perhaps that was the key to my healing. But then a conversation went on in my mind as if there were two people inside it. (Little did I realize that Satan was already at work in my thought-life, trying to rob me of the healing God wanted to give me. At that point, had someone tried to warn me, I wouldn't have believed in any doctrine about the devil anyway.)

The negative voice said, "Where did you ever hear that God heals today? You never heard anything like that in church, did you?"

I had to admit I hadn't heard of healings taking place today, except through medical science. But then I thought of another Scripture Barbara had read to me just the night before: "Jesus Christ the same yesterday, and to day, and for ever" (Hebrews 13:8).

The two Scriptures were like nuggets of gold, and when I put them together, I decided God wanted to heal me. My reasoning went something like this: "OK, that must mean Jesus is capable of doing the same things now that He did when He was on earth. If Jesus is not dead—and they say He rose from the dead—then that means He still can do anything if I ask Him and believe He will do it." It was an interesting thought—even an exciting one.

I knew my Bible was on the table next to the couch where I was sitting. I fumbled around until I found it, then picked it up and held it near me. As I mused about the different Scriptures, my engineer's mind began snapping into gear. In school I'd learned how to use textbooks. We would take the axioms, theorems and postulates, bring them into the laboratory, and try to prove or discredit them. That's exactly how I intended to handle the Bible.

I didn't know how to use King James English. All I knew was that in church I'd always heard an "amen" tacked onto the end of a prayer. So, clutching the Bible, I spoke to God with all the sincerity I could muster.

"God," I said, "if You are real, and if the Bible is true, I stand on these two Scriptures: Anything I ask in prayer, believing, I will receive—and Jesus is the same now as He was when on earth and He can do the same miracles. I'm asking You for sight in at least one eye so that I will be able to read Your Word. Amen."

I knew the answer to this prayer would require nothing short of an absolute miracle. My blindness was due to my disease which had attacked the optic nerve. The doctors had told me that the nerve was severely damaged; if I regained any sight at all, it would be only the peripheral (outside) vision. That meant engineering was out. I would never again be able to see the intricate detail of electrical blueprints. I would never again be able to read, for that matter, as reading is done with the macular (center) portion of the eye, and the doctors said there was no possibility that this would be restored. So I knew that if I received my sight, I'd be compelled to believe in the reality of God.

The beginning of a miracle-filled life started two weeks after that simple prayer. It was on a Saturday morning in the late fall; Barbara and I had been out riding and had stopped at a favorite park where I'd played during my childhood. Taking my suggestion that we go for a walk, Barbara got out and came around to my side to help me. Then she took me by the hand and told me when to step over something or when to sidestep to avoid a rock or a rough spot. I was trying very hard to smile and be pleasant because I wanted Barbara to be happy. As we walked through the park hand in hand, we reminisced about our life together before MS.

The first year we were married had been sheer bliss. I'd sit at dinner with Barbara and say, "You know this is too wonderful, don't you? People just aren't this happy. Something is going to happen." At the time, I didn't realize how prophetic my words were.

Barbara and I had grown up in the same town. I'd taken her out once when she was fourteen, but she had silly ideas about marriage and I wasn't interested then. It wasn't until we had both been away at different colleges that we met again, and fell in love. By this time, I was ready to accept her "silly" ideas about marriage—and I was overjoyed when she agreed to be my wife.

At the reception after our wedding, someone ran up to me and said, "Come with me. Hurry up! There's a double rainbow outside I want you to see." It had been a beautiful, sunshiny day in late August, but a ten-minute shower brought out the rainbows. Someone else shouted, "Yeah, that's right. They're out there! That's God's blessing on your marriage!" But I was too boozed up to bother with what I thought were people's fantasies.

We had been successful in getting good jobs too. Both of us were doing exactly what we'd always dreamed of. My wife was working for two topnotch psychiatrists, and I was employed with a consulting firm in electrical engineering. I was getting raises almost every month, and Barbara was making good money too. We had the world by the tail.

But now the bottom had fallen out!

As we walked in the park that day, I could picture in my mind the lake we were near. Barbara's dad and I had fished there many times during the past summer. We were approaching an open green when I suddenly jerked Barbara's hand. As she looked at me, startled, I blinked my eyes, then covered them with my hand and prayed I wasn't dreaming. Sure enough, something had happened!

When I uncovered my eyes, I could see a sign that said NO FISHING. I closed my eyes again and the sign disappeared. When I opened them again, it was still there.

A knot formed in my throat. "Barbara!" I gasped. "That sign!"

"Wh—what about it?" she stammered.

"That sign says NO FISHING!" I declared. "NO FISHING!"

"You mean you can *see* it?" Barbara asked incredulously.

"Yes, honey, I *really can!* I can see it! I can see it!"

Barbara and I fell into each other's arms and wept for joy. A miracle had happened to *me*, Doug Foley! God had restored my sight, and I didn't even know Him yet! It was too wonderful to believe.

When we had recovered from the initial shock and excitement, I ran over to the car all by myself and we raced home to shout the news to my folks. What rejoicing took place in the Foley household that day!

Two days later Barbara and I packed up and moved back to our own little love nest. There was no need to burden my family any longer.

Chapter Three

CITY SLICKERS 'N' COUNTRY FOLKS

Of what use is pride to Me? None whatsoever. But I, the Lord, know how to bring down the lofty looks of men. I know how to make men usable. My way is simple: "Except ye be converted, and become as little children. . . ." *

I work in strange ways; onlookers may marvel and even smile at My methods of dealing with proud, self-sufficient men. But My ways are effective.

Though I knew multiple sclerosis is medically incurable, I was now beginning to wonder if God was going to heal me completely.

The doctors had said I'd never be able to read even

---
* Matthew 18:3.

if some sight *did* return; but I could read anything! The center of one eye had completely cleared and the other was beginning to let in light.

Yet, other symptoms of MS were hanging on stubbornly. I decided I'd better get serious about God.

Pete was still in the hospital when Barbara and I decided to visit his church, but he arranged for his wife to take us to the Saturday night service. I wasn't used to keeping company with Christians, and I wasn't sure I wanted to begin. I'd always thought of Christians as meek, namby-pamby people, continually turning the other cheek to accept somebody's guff. But Pete's wife was human—not the "goody-two-shoes" I'd expected. When some driver in another car would do something foolish, she'd say disgustedly, "Did you see that? What's the matter with people anyway?!" She was a frank, down-to-earth woman, and I felt quite comfortable in her company.

The church service was held in a little community center. When we arrived, we were somewhat surprised to be escorted through a poolroom.

"A poolroom!" I exclaimed under my breath. "I thought we were going to church!" But we followed Pete's wife as she led us to the back and up some stairs into a small meeting room on the second floor.

I don't believe I'd ever felt so badly out of place. The other people there looked like a handful of country folks ready for a hoedown. Barbara and I were dressed the way fashion-conscious city people do.

Barbara was elegant in her black, smartly tailored suit. Her blond hair complemented high cheekbones and a sharp chin. She did not blend in easily with the wallpaper or with these women in their simple, clean, cotton dresses.

The love between a high-strung Swedish mother and a fun-loving Irish dad had combined to make me a ruddy-complexioned, medium-framed guy. Nothing special marked me except for a pug nose, plenty of pride, and high ambition. Snobbery told me these people were definitely not our type. We were very much aware of "in" things, and obviously these people weren't in the know.

It was evident that some of the men had put in a hard day's work and hadn't bothered to change clothes before coming to the service. Where I was brought up, you just didn't go to church without dressing up. In fact, the church our family attended had seemed to be more of a "house of fashion" than a place of worship.

We were led to a row of folding chairs in the middle of the room, where we sat down and waited for the service to begin. For better or for worse, we were now trapped.

At 7:30 a woman wearing a bright red hat began jubilantly playing the portable organ up front. She appeared to be an accomplished musician, and her lively playing accompanied equally spirited singing. They sang "There's Power in the Blood" and "Count Your Blessings," clapping their hands in time to the music. I didn't really know what to think about singing with such gusto in church. I almost felt embarrassed; yet something in my spirit wanted to join right in. My mind won the battle that night, however, and

I didn't participate with the enthusiasm that the others exhibited.

Between songs, people would pop up and tell what the Lord had done for them during the week. They talked as if they knew Jesus as well as I know Barbara. I couldn't understand this; He'd always been just a storybook character to me.

At one point, the organist stood up and gave her testimony. She said she had been a concert pianist until her elbow was crushed in an automobile accident. She said her crippled arm had ended her career, since she could no longer reach the keys to play concert pieces. Then her face lit up as she said, "But Jesus healed me. I have pictures of myself before and after I was healed to prove it!"

I'd never heard anything like this. As I sat there trying to digest it, suddenly I realized that the sermon had already begun.

The preacher was a woman. When she had greeted us on our arrival, she was quiet and soft-spoken, and her gentle smile and manner made us feel welcome. But when this fragile little lady began to preach, it came out the way steam burst out of my wife's pressure cooker the time she removed the toggler too soon.

The sermon had barely begun when Barbara started poking in her purse. I heard her sniffle and blow her nose. A little later, she dug into her purse again for a fistful of Kleenex.

"You all right?"

"Yes." She tried to grin at me.

Ten minutes passed. The preaching continued.

Tears streamed down Barbara's face, and her mascara began to run. My wife was always so poised. In college she had won a contest judged on the basis of beauty, poise and personality. But the way she was acting now, no one would have believed it!

"What's the matter, honey?" I whispered softly.

She shook her head and whispered back, "I can't talk now."

The preaching flowed on, and so did my wife's tears and mascara. Her face was streaked, and I was uncomfortable and annoyed, to say the least.

"Pull yourself together," I finally growled.

But it was no use. She kept on sobbing, and the harder I tried to stop her, the more of a spectacle we made.

The preaching was all about Jesus. I couldn't see anything upsetting about it. We were told how the blood of Jesus washes away our sins, and that through His death on the Cross, Jesus bought us and gave us eternal life. The preacher said that when we invite Jesus into our hearts, the same resurrection power that raised Him from the dead comes into our hearts, and we are "born again."

There was that phrase again!

The sermon lasted about twenty minutes. At the end of it, we were invited to the altar to receive the gift of salvation.

Well, Barbara finally stopped sobbing and fidgeting. But before I could become too relieved about that, she was tramping all over my nicely polished shoes, pushing her way past me to the altar—her face still streaked with make-up, here eyes puffed and red.

I could have died! There was my wife standing in front of the minister, while I sat in my seat completely mortified.

We'd always done things together, and I wanted to keep it that way. When we were married, I'd promised myself that I'd do my best to keep us together in everything. So as the people sang the last verse of "Just as I Am," I joined my wife. Not knowing what to expect next, I stood with her quietly, feeling a little apprehensive about the whole thing.

When the singing stopped, the minister said, "Repeat after me." And we prayed: "Dear Jesus, I know I'm a sinner. Please forgive me and come into my heart. I believe Your blood washed away my sins, and I believe God the Father raised You from the dead. I accept You as my Lord and Savior and I take the gift of salvation. Amen."

There were puddles of tears around my wife, but I was no longer upset by her crying. I was beginning to understand what she had evidently been feeling all through the service. Pride wouldn't let me cry, although I wanted to. It was as though I'd just entered a new world—and I had!

"This must be what that 'born-again' thing is all about," I thought.

Somehow I knew this experience was going to change our lives. I couldn't explain it, but I knew something had happened deep inside of me when I prayed aloud. But what I didn't know was that being born again was just the beginning. Growing up was a lot more interesting—and a lot harder.

Chapter Four

PLAYING SECOND FIDDLE TO JESUS

The problem of pride is beyond all human help. No man, by strength of determination, has ever been able to crush the head of this viper. But think not that the problem is hopeless. Only recognize that it is "not by might, nor by power, but by my spirit. . . ." *

The first changes came rapidly. Our interest in the person of Jesus Christ mushroomed. Bible reading became important. We learned that all food is good when it's sanctified by prayer, so we began asking God's blessings at mealtime. We saved money for offerings instead of liquor, and lost interest in nightclubbing. And tithing was the beginning of learning to put God first in everything.

Nearly every other weekend throughout that win-

---
* Zechariah 4:6.

ter, we travelled a hundred miles to sit under the ministry through which we were born again. Heavy snowstorms didn't deter us. We never considered that we might attend a church nearer our home. There were churches nearby, of course—but as far as we knew, the only *real Christians* in the whole world were in that little place two hours' drive from Hartford.

We had no idea that January 15, 1967, would mark another very wonderful milestone in our growth as Christians. Exactly three months earlier, we had met Jesus as Lord and Savior. And prior to that I had met Him as Healer. But this day was to bring us into an even greater dimension of spiritual knowledge.

The day was clear and beautiful, and we enjoyed our drive to church for the morning worship service. Our new friends welcomed us with smiles and open arms. Soon the service started. By now, we were used to the way things were done and we participated wholeheartedly in the jubilant singing and hand-clapping.

After the service, the lady minister invited us to have dinner with her. We accepted the invitation gladly. Both of us had lots of questions stored up, and this would be a good opportunity to get them answered.

After dinner, the conversation turned to the subject of the Holy Spirit. "You know," the pastor said, "I'm very excited about these days. Did either of you ever read in the Bible about the outpouring of the Holy Spirit we're to expect in the last days?"

"No, I don't believe so," I admitted. "Where *is* that?"

She turned to Joel 2:28 and showed us where God said, "I will pour out my spirit upon all flesh."

"But didn't that happen on the day of Pentecost?" I asked.

"Yes," the pastor replied, "but it's for us too." Quickly she flipped over to Acts 2:39 and showed us that the Spirit is promised to "all that are afar off, even as many as the Lord our God shall call."

"I'm not sure I understand," I said after some thought. "Both of us already know Jesus, but you seem to be saying there's something more."

"There is!" she replied. "It's called the baptism in the Holy Spirit."

"And what will that do for us?" Barbara asked eagerly.

"It'll give you *power*," she replied. "Power to overcome Satan and fleshly desires so your life will be a witness for Jesus."

"We could use power like that," I commented. "How do we get it?"

Again the pastor found an answer in the Bible. I was tempted to smile; apparently she thought the answer to every question was in that Book!

She showed us Luke 11:13: "If ye then, being evil, know how to give good gifts unto your children: how much more shall your heavenly Father give the Holy Spirit to them that ask him?"

"See," she pointed out, "all you've got to do is *ask*."

"OK," I said, "but how will we know when it happens?"

"Oh, that's easy," she replied. "It says in Acts 2:4 that 'they were all filled with the Holy Ghost, and began to speak with other tongues, as the Spirit gave them utterance.' And it's no different today. The Holy Spirit will give you power to pray in tongues."

"Tongues?" Barbara and I chorused. "What's that?"

"Praying in tongues is speaking to God in a language you don't know," she smiled. "This is the initial sign that Jesus gives as evidence of being baptized in His Spirit."

"You mean a person receiving the Spirit will begin to speak in tongues without even trying?" I asked.

"Well, not exactly without trying. In John 7:37, Jesus said, 'If any man thirst, let him come unto me, and drink.' And verse thirty-nine makes it clear that Jesus was talking about receiving the Holy Spirit when He said that. So, you see, we have some responsibility in the matter too. We must drink. As we drink in the Holy Spirit, or *breathe* Him in, we will then receive power to worship in tongues. But it's up to us to *use* that power. The Holy Spirit won't speak in tongues *for* you, but He'll give you the power."

"But I thought you said the power of the Spirit was for spiritual warfare," I objected.

"That's right," she replied. "But speaking in tongues is God's way of sustaining that power in you. First Corinthians 14:4 says, 'He that speaketh in an unknown tongue edifieth himself.' You keep yourself built up by regular prayer in tongues—and then when the time comes for witnessing or warfare, you'll not be lacking power."

"That sounds great!" I commented. "Why haven't we heard of this before?"

"Well, you must remember that there are many who don't grasp this teaching," she replied. "Some churches actually *forbid* speaking in tongues, even though the Apostle Paul tells us very plainly in First Corinthians 14:39 that tongues are not to be forbidden. Of course there *are* regulations for the public use of tongues. Obviously, you can't allow everybody to speak in tongues in a church service, just as you can't allow everyone to preach. According to First Corinthians 14:27, tongues are permissible in each service, but they must always be interpreted."

Barbara and I were fascinated. We had never before heard such teaching but we were both hungry for more of the Lord. Since the church was right next door, we politely excused ourselves and went over to pray to be baptized in the Holy Spirit. Our hearts were pounding with anticipation.

We must have prayed for half an hour. While kneeling, I had an awesome sense of the presence of God in the building. He was no longer some far-away idea, but a God Who could feel my joy—and my sorrow! He would always be there to take care of me and direct me. All my intellect suddenly seemed worthless. I felt like a small child who raises his arms and says, "Please, Daddy, pick me up."

I heard the church door open, then shut, and quiet footsteps tiptoed toward us. "Has Jesus baptized you yet?" a voice asked. It was the pastor.

"No, not yet," we said. Then the minister prayed that Jesus would baptize me in the Holy Spirit. She had prayed only a minute, when something strange began to happen.

I began praying and a strange language came spilling out, with rrr's rolling over my tongue. Great joy began to well up within me, flowing out like rivers!

It was so easy to worship God! I felt completely free of pride and self-conciousness! I just wanted to praise Him and praise Him! There were no more inhibitions about raising my hands toward heaven and adoring God.

A minute later, the same thing happened to Barbara. The whole building seemed to be flooded with joy. God must have opened the windows of heaven that day, as His Spirit came *pouring* down upon us. For three hours it poured—and we prayed in tongues the whole time! There was reverence—yet, at the same time, a tremendous joy and holy laughter.

After this experience, it was no longer any mystery to us why the crowds on the day of Pentecost accused the 120 of being drunk on "new wine" after the Lord had baptized them in the Spirit. Anybody would have thought the same of us!

For a while the going was great, and I thought all my troubles were over. Praying in tongues did indeed prove to be a great source of spiritual strength, as the pastor had said it would be—and I felt sure I'd "arrived." Little did I know how much more work God had to do on me!

The first problem was that I didn't understand the depth of my own "inner dilemma." I *thought* I had surrendered everything to God, but I wasn't yet aware of my biggest problem: *pride and self-sufficency*. And being unaware of its existence, I couldn't yield to God on that point.

My second problem was my supposition that being born again and baptized in the Spirit would take care of all the difficulties I had. I didn't see that this was just the beginning, and that God wanted to teach me to *walk* in the Spirit—daily. Neither did I take into account the weakness of my own fleshly mind, nor the power of the devil. Consequently, I had a lot to learn.

I'll never forget the "chair-squirming days." By spring, Barbara and I had discovered several groups of Spirit-baptized Christians that met in nearby churches. So we began "meeting hopping," trying to soak up all the teaching we could. But the more teaching I received, the more uncomfortable I became. I can't quite explain what happened to me; maybe I was trying to absorb too much too fast. All I know is that I soon began to feel as though God were telling me, "Do this! Do that! Don't do this! Don't do that!"

Then Satan began his subtle temptations, suggesting to me that Christianity is nothing but a set of *dos* and *don'ts*—something I had nicely done without previously, and could be very happy without now. I had always been my own boss, and I wondered whether even *God* had a right to expect that kind of subservience. Surely I had a *few* rights!

My wife, on the other hand, apparently had no trouble at all in accepting the mild Christian discipline we were receiving. She soaked in the teaching like a sponge. But not me. I gradually stopped reading the Bible, especially when I learned I'd be held responsible for the knowledge I received from it. Foolishly, I was beginning to think that the less I knew, the better off I'd be. I didn't know my ignorance could get me in trouble.

I grew more and more nervous as my spirit and my flesh warred against each other. While in such a divided state of mind, I began to take out my spite on Barbara, yelling at her and saying unkind things.

At home, books about Jesus and teachings on the manifestations of the Holy Spirit filled the shelves and were scattered on the coffee table and bedstand. They were even in the bathroom! For Barbara, reading replaced television—and I soon felt that it was beginning to replace *me*. It seemed she spent hours with her nose in a book. I became angry that God was getting more of her time and interest than I was, and that I had to play second fiddle to Jesus. Soon I actually became jealous of God, feeling that He and I were vying for the affections of the same woman.

One evening, a Christian couple stopped by our home for a visit. Before they left, Barbara suggested that we gather around the kitchen table for prayer. During that prayer, the Lord spoke to me through a prophetic message from one of our guests.

"Give Me your wife. Give Me your wife, for I am a jealous God!" *

I knew it was the Lord all right. Tears filled my eyes, and I sensed the presence of God as I sat there. I was afraid, but I was still resistant.

Barbara meant more to me than anything or anyone else, including God, and I couldn't bear to think of

---
* See Exodus 20:5.

letting her go. All our struggles had brought us very close together, and I had become very dependent upon her. I knew I had her on a pedestal in my mind, and I wanted her to stay there. I was in mental anguish as the Holy Spirit dealt with me there at the table. I'm sure everyone could see the agony on my face.

Some Christian friends had told me that God always wants us to put Him first and give up anything or anyone else who might be dearer to us than He is. *But*, I had been assured, He always gives them right back. It was a nice theory, I thought, but I couldn't buy it. I was afraid that if I gave God my wife, He'd keep her!

The Spirit was still heavy upon me, however. Minutes seemed like hours. Finally I cried out, "OK, Lord! Take her!"

With that, I felt an invisible shovel scooping out the idolatry of my soul. I gasped and grabbed at my chest as a sharp pain stabbed into my heart. Something was happening. My wife was being moved out of the "Holy Place," and Jesus was moving in. Oh, God! What had I done? What had I done?

When it was all over and our guests had left, Barbara and I solemnly got ready for bed. I wondered if she felt as strange as I did. Though I couldn't define it, something was different between us. I felt alone, even though she was with me. When I asked Barbara if she felt different, however, all she could tell me was that she loved me much more since Jesus had come into our lives than she had ever dreamed possible before. And I could tell that she meant it.

I still loved her too, but I couldn't understand this "different" feeling. As time went on, I even began to feel guilty about not loving her "like I used to." By that, I guess I meant that I no longer idolized her. Instead of being buoyed up by this experience, as I should have been, I began to sink in guilt and self-condemnation.

Looking for a way out of my misery, I finally convinced Barbara that we should attend a nearby church I had picked out. The sermons there were much easier for me to bear than those we'd been hearing lately. The church was more like a social club than a church, and it served as an escape from all the spiritual pressure I'd been under.

Within six months after we began attending that church, I was back into my old life-style. Since Barbara wasn't pulling the same way I was, our relationship continued to deteriorate. I was entering a spiritual blindness as dark as my physical one had been, and it would take something drastic to open my eyes. Barbara knew it. Privately she stormed the gates of heaven with her prayers for me, especially praying in tongues. And when the day drew near for God to turn me around, the Spirit said to her, "It's coming. Hang on tight!"

And it came. . . .

It started with a weak feeling in my legs, which gradually increased. By the fifth day, I couldn't walk without assistance.

I should have known better than to stray away from the Lord. God's Word contains the clear warning, "Sin no more, lest a worst thing come unto thee" (John 5:14). But all I could think of was, "I quit smoking, Lord. What more do You want?!" (I had formerly smoked more than two packs of cigarettes a day, and I honestly thought I had done a great thing by sacrificing this vice that I thoroughly enjoyed.)

Every day my wife would come to me and say, "Honey, we both know what God is requiring. Please give yourself to Him." But I would not give in. And every day I grew a little worse.

By the tenth day I was as helpless as a baby. Completely immobilized from the waist down, I could neither move a muscle nor feel a pinprick.

Again my wife prodded me. "Honey, you've got to give in. You *must* give yourself to Jesus—*all* of you. Don't hold back anymore. Please! I'm afraid of what will happen to you if you don't give in. He's the only One who can help you now."

She came through. God wanted more than my cigarettes—and more than my wife. He wanted everything—all of me. He wanted me to hold back nothing from Him.

I'd been angry and cursing up until then, but now I broke. "OK," I gritted my teeth and sobbed. I had to strain to make the words come out: "I yield! I yield!"

Heavy weeping broke from my spirit, and then I grew calm and relaxed. The next morning I could detect an ever-so-slight movement in my legs. I had begun to improve! By now, however, the wheels had been set in motion for my hospitalization. Thanks to my stubbornness, the worst was yet to come.

Chapter Five

FROM 200 POUNDS TO 120

Must I humble you again? Yes, I will do it as often as I must. Pomp must be brought down to the grave,* and only I can do it lovingly.

I was sent to Boston—a full two hours' drive from home—to a special hospital for MS victims. There they put me on extremely high doses of ACTH (adrenocorticotropic hormone), far exceeding the usual maximum dosage. Some people become euphoric on this drug, but I became so depressed and irrational that, at one point, I picked up a tray and nearly clobbered an aide simply because her voice irritated me.

---
* See Isaiah 14:11.

In a few weeks' time my weight jumped from 165 pounds to more than 200. The bloating effect of the drug made me feel as if leather belts were buckled all over my body and some tormentor were continually yanking them tight, then loosening them again. And there was the vexing sensation of lying on squishy little balls of jelly just under my skin.

I kept thinking the treatments would soon be over, and I finally asked the doctor how long I would be on the drug. His reply was that, since I had such unusually high doses for so long, I would have to take maintenance doses of ACTH for the rest of my life! He felt that if I did not, I might have an MS attack that could very well paralyze me permanently from the neck down.

The horror of what I was hearing was almost unbearable! I didn't know which was worse—the sickness or the cure. But I did know that nobody could spend the rest of his life feeling the way I did and remain sane. There would be no use in living any more. I knew there was only one solution. . . .

Every day for a month I struggled into the small bathroom near my bed and prayed. It was a taxing effort, but my legs had improved enough so that I could make it if I took it very slowly.

"Lord," I would plead with all my heart, "I can't stand it! Please, please get me off this drug somehow. I don't care how You do it—just get me off!"

As I prayed I recalled how, during the past winter, the Lord had shown me His ability to take care of "impossible" situations. Barbara and I had been driving over country roads made slippery by an ice storm. As we came over the crest of a particularly steep hill, the car slid into a snow bank and became solidly stuck. I grumbled loudly—but then we looked down the hill and saw that an oil truck and a car had spun around on the ice and were stuck crosswise on the road. Had we started down that steep, icy hill, there would have been no way to avoid hitting the truck or the car.

We thanked God for stopping us—but then we began to wonder how we could keep from freezing. We were not dressed for a hike in subfreezing temperatures. No help was in sight, and we couldn't expect any for hours. Barbara suggested prayer. I admit I thought it was a dumb idea, but I couldn't come up with a better one.

"You do it," I grumbled.

"Lord, first move the oil truck," she prayed, "then the car. Then have someone get us out of here, please. In Jesus' name. Amen."

Barbara had hardly finished praying when we saw the oil truck being pushed out of the way by a highway truck. Then the car was moved. As soon as it had driven off, a pickup truck came from the other direction and slid to a stop beside us. The driver got out of his truck, put chains on his wheels, and backed up behind our car. Hitching a chain to our rear bumper, he pulled us out of the snow bank, and off he went. All this was accomplished in fifteen minutes flat!

As I prayed in the bathroom, I recalled that wonderful answer to Barbara's prayer, and also remembered how God had restored my sight in answer to my own feeble attempt to pray. Those memories encouraged me to believe that God would get me off that drug *somehow*. Within a few days He did—but the "somehow" nearly killed me!

It seems that the ACTH had drained my system of certain nutrients which had not been adequately replaced. The imbalance caused clotting of the blood in my veins. Three clots went to my lungs as pulmonary emboli, one passing through the heart into an artery, causing a coronary infarction. After an operation on my legs to tie off the veins through which the clots were travelling, I was taken off the ACTH (as I'd prayed!) and sent to the Intensive Care Unit.

Trained warriors in white battled the death angel around the clock. Intensive Care was a busy place. Nurses scooted around almost mechanically from one sick bed to another. Most of the patients seemed to be just a heartbeat from heaven—or hell, as the case may have been; the way some patients twisted and contorted, kicked and scratched, one could easily believe they were fighting demons trying to drag them off to the gates of hades.

Lights were on in Intensive Care around the clock, since there were no windows in the room. Everything was sterile white.

Pneumonia set in to complicate my condition, and my fever rose so high that I was delirious much of the time. To lower my temperature, they put me on a plastic refrigerated pad. Sometimes my chills would shake the whole bed.

When I drifted off to sleep, I often had the horrible, weird dreams that go along with fever. I remember being jostled awake once; when I looked up, it was as if I were at the bottom of a well, looking up through the water at fuzzy faces peering down at me. I vaguely recollected hearing glass smash, but didn't realize I had torn down the bottles of intravenous fluid and yanked the needles out of my arm. I was being scolded like a naughty child as the fluid fed the floor instead of me. After that, my arms were strapped down.

My illness and the sudden withdrawal of ACTH caused my weight to drop from 200 to 120 pounds; wrinkled, jaundiced skin draped my bones. I felt like a codfish being thrown on a slab when the orderlies plopped me on a board to weigh me. All my dignity was gone, like so much garbage. It didn't seem possible that I'd ever be normal again.

Barbara told me later that, when I was brought into Intensive Care, a nurse came over to her with great pity in her eyes, and said in a heavy Irish brogue, "There are no babies, are there?" She seemed relieved to know that children would not be left fatherless. This was only one of the several indications that the doctors and nurses thought it was all over for me.

Finally I was moved from Intensive Care to a private room—not because I was showing any improvement, but because I wasn't. There was no more that could be done for me in Intensive Care, so I was sent away to my lonely corner to die quietly.

"This is hell. This is *real hell!*" I would say to any visitors brave enough to come into my room. They would look at me sadly, not wanting to raise any false hopes.

Visitors could stay only a short while since I could tolerate very little disturbance before beginning to hyperventilate. Barbara's presence seemed to ease me, however, so she would stay.

Barbara came into my room one morning after I had had a particularly bad night and was too sick even to grumble. Realizing I didn't want to talk, she just sat by the bed and held my hand while I dozed off. Suddenly I awoke with a start.

"What's wrong, honey?" Barbara asked fearfully, jumping to her feet.

"I had a vision!" I replied in astonishment.

"A vision? What did you see?" she asked.

"I saw a room," I told her. "It was some kind of council room. There was a long table in it, and twelve men in long white robes were sitting on one side of the table, facing me. Then the second one from the end got up, came around in front of the table, and spoke to me."

"Well, what did he say?" Barbara pressed.

"With his finger pointing at me, he said, 'Don't you ever tell anyone again that what you are going through is hell. This is NOTHING compared to what hell is *really* like!' Then the vision disappeared and I woke up."

Barbara seemed lost for words. All she could do was squeeze my hand tenderly and look at me with those understanding eyes.

I lay in the hospital for four months. Barbara made the two-hour drive from home every weekend. How I looked forward to her coming! I knew she was praying for me. Since the blood clots had hit, I had become too tired and too sick to pray for myself any more. But I could rest assured that she was releasing prayer-power on my behalf. I could feel strength coming out of her when she sat by my bedside.

I had no way of knowing that Barbara was going through a lonely wilderness herself. Because I had discontinued fellowship with other born-again Christians before I landed in the hospital, no one was sharing the burden with her. No one was around to comfort her in the Lord. No one knew of the spiritual warfare she was fighting, as she pled with God for my life. Certainly she could not confide in the doctors; more than likely they would have thought her to be a real loony-tune had she attempted to explain to them that pride and stubbornness had gotten me into this mess.

At one point when she was alone in prayer, Barbara went into a kind of spiritual travail—something like the agony that a woman goes through when she gives birth to a child. As she allowed the Holy Spirit to intercede in prayer through her, she experienced the "groanings which cannot be uttered" that Paul spoke about in Romans 8:26. Her suffering must have been similar to that experienced by the Apostle Paul for the sake of the backslidden Galatians. He addressed them as "my little children, for whom I am again suffering birth pangs until Christ is completely and permanently formed (molded) within you!" (Galatians 4:19, Amplified Bible). I had already been born again, but it was as though the Holy Spirit, through my wife, was travailing to bring me forth again—this time with Christ fully formed in me! Finally, though, she could struggle no more; it was time to release me—time to take her hands off me and allow God freedom to carry out His will. She saw that her previous prayers had been "tying God's hands." She felt led of the Holy Spirit to pray, "Lord, take his life if You want to. But if You let him live, then make him whole and give him a purpose. I release him completely to You."

That prayer was a turning point in my illness. From that time on, I began to see little improvements. But the improvements were so small that on certain days I wondered if I were making any progress at all. It was on one of those days that the consulting neurologist walked in with his retinue of eager, inquisitive students.

"Oh, no!" I thought. I wished I had the strength to slide under the sheets in the hope they wouldn't see me.

"Please go away," I urged the doctor in a weak voice. "I'm too tired for experiments today."

It was no use. His purpose that day was not to help me, but to give the students a first-hand look at a trophy-winning specimen. Too sick to put up an argument, I submitted to their poking, pin-pricking, and feather-tickling. At least fifteen of them had a crack at me. Then it was their teacher's turn.

"I'm going to pick both your legs off the bed," he announced. "I want you to hold them there when I let go. Do you understand?"

I nodded that I did, and up went my legs. "Hold them now," he ordered.

Flop! They thumped on the bed again.

"Good," he said. "Very good!" And they all marched out, assignment completed.

"How stupid!" I thought disgustedly. "*Good!*" But then the absurdity of the scene hit my funny bone and

I began to chuckle. I laughed myself right off to sleep.

When I awoke, Barbara was sitting by my side.

"What's new?" I asked.

"Oh, Cathy was over this week," she said. "I haven't seen her since you and I were married."

Cathy was a girl who attended a Greek Orthodox church. She had been Barbara's confidant when they were in college.

"Cathy asked me what was going on in my life, and we got to talking about Jesus and the baptism in the Holy Spirit," she continued. "You'll never believe what happened.

"She asked me to speak in tongues and, since we can use tongues as a sign to unbelievers,* I did." She paused to make sure she had my attention. "I *spoke in Greek*. She told me I prayed a prayer they say in the Greek Orthodox church every week!"

"You *did?*" I replied in amazement. Since I'd been in my backslidden state, I had decided that speaking in tongues was just a lot of jibberish. But I knew Barbara couldn't speak a word of Greek, and now she was telling me she'd actually prayed in that language —and that one who *knew* Greek had understood it!

What a faith-builder *that* was! I felt ashamed that I'd ever doubted the reality of the beautiful prayer language God had given us on that day when we were baptized in the Holy Spirit.

"I have more news," Barbara said. "I've decided that you're going home!"

My eyes lit up for an instant. But then I realized

---
* 1 Corinthians 14:22.

what a crazy idea *that* was. "How can I go home when I'm like this?" I asked.

"I've already talked to the doctor about it," she replied. And she went on to explain that the blood specialist had told her how to give me the bloodthinners needed to keep my blood from coagulating, and how to drain and care for the incision on my leg that still hadn't healed properly. He said all lights were green for my going home, as far as he was concerned —provided Barbara would carry out his instructions.

It sounded encouraging. But when Barbara talked with the neurologist, it was another story. "Definitely not! Definitely not!" he insisted. "There are many tests that we still have to do."

But Barbara felt the Lord was advising, "Definitely yes!" And that made it a majority! She quit her job in order to give me full-time attention, and a few days later I signed out of the hospital—with twenty-seven different drugs in my suitcase.

Chapter Six

EVERY GOOD GARDEN NEEDS FERTILIZER

> *"After all I've been through," you think, "surely He must have something great in store for me!" Ah, but what is worse in My eyes than he who thinks himself worthy of some great honor—whereas the pride of all men is but dung in my sight?* *

Pills, pills, pills! I thought I heard myself rattle when my wife turned me over on the bed. Red ones and blue ones, green ones and yellow ones, square ones and round ones, triangles and rectangles. The pills, liquid medications, syringes, needles, thermometers, basins, and bedpans filled the top of the kitchen counter.

I had finally made it home. As we had pulled up in

---
* See Psalm 83:9,10.

front of the house, some of the neighbors had come out to greet me and wish me well. I was so embarrassed at my condition, I just wanted them to go away. But instead of going away, they carried me in and plopped my skinny, helpless body on the chaise lounge in the middle of the living room. Barbara had made it into a hospital bed, equipped with soft sheepskin to ease my bony bottom and a rubber ring to keep my tailbone from piercing through my skin. I was like a helpless baby.

"Open up," I heard, as Barbara pushed a big wad of gum into my mouth. The chewing relaxed my squeamish stomach while she changed the dressing on my leg.

Next it was time for my bath. Most of the nurses in the hospital had been too embarrassed to wash me properly, and my condition had become quite obnoxious by the time I got home. It was good to smell clean again.

Gospel records played morning, noon, and night as Barbara worked around the house, fed me, and took care of me. An atmosphere of faith filled our home as the music played. The songs lifted my spirit and reminded me of God's love and mercy. I believe this music, as much as anything else, helped toward my recovery.

Every day Barbara would read the Scriptures to me. The more she read, the more I improved. It was like taking medicine all day long: regular pills and "Gos-pills"!

At first Barbara read to me from the Bible only a few minutes each day. As the days passed, she increased the dosage to fifteen minutes a day, then to half an hour, and finally up to two hours throughout the day. At the time I didn't realize what was happening; but since that time, I've found the explanation in Proverbs 4:20-22: "My son, attend to my words; incline thine ear unto my sayings. Let them not depart from thine eyes; keep them in the midst of thine heart. For they are life unto those that find them, and health [the Hebrew word is "medicine"] to all their flesh." I was taking God's medicine! And sure enough, it was beginning to heal my flesh!

I could feel myself growing stronger. Stringy, spaghetti-like veins, which had collapsed because so much blood had been taken from them while I was in the hospital, began puffing back to normal size. The Word of God healed me from the inside out. The healing started in my spirit, and finally I saw the results in my body.

But things did not run smoothly for us all the time. One morning I awoke to find the whole room in a spin. When I closed my eyes for escape, there was no relief. Everything continued spinning until I felt nauseated and frightened. When I told Barbara, she called a local doctor who had been following my case, but he said there was nothing anyone could do.

The dizziness continued for a month. Praying did no good; reading the Bible did no good; crying did no good. Probably I'd still be spinning if God hadn't revealed to Barbara what to do.

She had been reading the Scriptures, and one sentence seemed to stand out: "When the bridegroom shall be taken from them . . . then shall they fast"

(Matthew 9:15). Neither of us knew much about fasting. This verse seemed to say that because Jesus was no longer with us in the flesh, fasting should be part of our Christian discipline. I was in no condition to fast, so Barbara decided she would do it *for* me. We had tried everything else we knew of and this was our last resort. For four days she took nothing but water.

The first day there was no improvement. Nor the second. But late that night I thought I was feeling better. Or was it only my imagination? The third day I was sure! By the fourth day, the dizziness was almost completely gone.

On the fifth day, Barbara couldn't take the fasting any longer. The Lord withdrew His strength, and she broke the fast when she got up that morning. But four days was all it required. My healing continued after the fast, and within a week I was over the dizziness completely.

After that, my faith in Jesus greatly increased. I began to believe that He was going to heal me completely. The more I thought about His healing power, the more ridiculous it seemed to be taking so many pills. One kind I was taking was to counteract the side-effects of a pill I was taking to counteract the side-effects of another pill! Finally I said, "Lord, You'll have to take care of me. I'm not taking these any more. If I die, I die. It's up to You." (Let me stress strongly here that I'm not telling any reader to stop taking prescribed medicine. I'm only relating what I did at a time when my faith—not presumption—was strong.)

A few weeks later, I was greatly improved. My color had returned, and I was gaining weight. Now that I was off medication, I was more alert and was becoming eager to walk.

One evening, while Barbara was in the kitchen preparing supper, a gentle Voice seemed to whisper to me, "Get up and walk." I wondered if this was only my imagination. I'd tried to walk many times before and had always failed. So I intended to be very cautious this time.

Knowing that Barbara would be busy with her cooking for some time, I decided to ask God for a little sign. "Lord, if that's You," I prayed, "have Barbara come in here right now."

No sooner had I uttered those words than there she was—standing in the middle of the living room—looking around with a scowl on her face, as if she'd forgotten something and was trying to remember what it was.

"What are *you* doing here?" I asked her, butterflies starting to flutter in my stomach.

"I don't know—" she replied, the bewildered look still on her face. "What *did* I come in here for anyway?"

"Well, *I* know," I blurted out. "Come over here and help me get up. God just told me to walk!"

With only a little argument, she helped me up. I tottered for a moment, then, thud! I hit the floor. But I knew in my spirit that I had heard from God, and I refused to be defeated.

"Get me up!" I demanded. "I'm going to try again."

Again she helped me to my feet *and I began to*

walk! It was tough going at first, and I walked like a waddling duck. But I *was* walking—that was what mattered. As I hobbled around the living room with Barbara's assistance, I could feel my leg muscles beginning to pull. They had shrunk so that my legs looked like straight sticks all the way up to my hips. My arms were the same way. All I needed now was exercise to get those muscles firmed up and working. God had touched me once more!

From that point, I gained in health and strength day after day. At first very laboriously, I began to do simple exercises in order to get my muscles back into shape. God had done His part, but some responsibility for my recovery rested with me. Several times each day, I'd hold onto the back of a chair while going up and down on my toes. This simple exercise brought out the calf muscles in a couple of weeks.

Soon I was independent enough for Barbara to go back to work without fearing the consequences of leaving me. I'd sleep most of the morning, since I was still far from strong; Barbara would come home at noon to prepare lunch for me, then go back to work. Being alone didn't bother me too much, since I could at least walk to the bathroom now, or go to the refrigerator when I became hungry. I still wasn't up to reading much on my own, but I *did* enjoy praying, and I spent quite a bit of time seeking the Lord's will for Barbara and me.

At first most of the conversations I had with God seemed rather one-sided; but there eventually came a day when God spoke to me very clearly. When Barbara came home from work that afternoon, she found me a little depressed.

"What's the matter, honey?" she asked with concern.

"God spoke to me today," I replied, staring at the floor glumly. "It sure wasn't what I was expecting, though." I had been thinking that with all I'd been through, there must be something important in store for me. I guess I must have thought that when God spoke to me, He would tell me how wonderful everything was going to be, how important I was, and how marvelously He intended to use me. (Old pride was a long way from being dead!)

"Well, what did He say?" Barbara asked.

"I'll tell you some other time."

"But why can't you tell me now?"

"You don't really want to know, do you?"

"Certainly I do! You're making me curious."

"OK," I blurted out. "He told me I was *dung*."

"Oh!" She stood there in stunned silence for a moment—then began to snicker.

"What's so funny?" I snapped. "You've got a weird sense of humor."

"I'm sorry, honey," Barbara replied, struggling to get control of herself. "It just seems funny that God would say that to anybody; are you sure it was the Lord?"

"Sure? He couldn't have said it more plainly if He had stood in front of me in the flesh and yelled in my face!"

"But why would He say that?" she asked, her smile fading now.

"I dunno," I replied, "but I've got a hunch it's got something to do with what Paul said in Romans 7:18."

"What's that?"

" 'In me . . . dwelleth no good thing.' "

She looked at me thoughtfully. "Could be," she replied after a moment's silence. Then, turning, she walked out to the kitchen to start supper.

I'm just grateful that God protected me from the full impact of what He'd said. I guess it's human nature to want to think we are worth at least a little more than dung, and it can be shattering to learn our true value. But God allowed just enough insight so that my spirit would be broken a little, but not totally shattered. It was a few weeks before I dared pray again. When I finally did gather the courage to talk to the Lord again, I spoke from a much lesser plane of self-importance.

As I waited on the Lord, He began gradually unfolding to me what He would do with my life if I would remain yielded to Him:

"You are a garden," He led me to see. "In your garden I have planted seeds. You must water these seeds with My Word. As you water them, they will begin to grow and bear fruit. The fruit is My character developing in you. But as the seeds sprout, so will the weeds, and I will deal with them by burning them out with the fire of the Holy Spirit. In time, the fruit will ripen and be abundant."

So it wasn't so bad after all to be dung! It makes the best fertilizer, and every good garden needs fertilizer!

Little by little, I began to understand what a close Friend I had in Jesus. Here was Someone Who would really level with me about my worst faults—and yet I never questioned His love for a moment.

One morning, I awoke to realize He had proved His love to me in another way. It had been a long time since I'd given my wife to God—but somewhere along the line He had given her back to me! I was finding out I loved her more dearly than ever before. Yet I was aware that she now had only second place in my life and that Jesus was in first. She wouldn't be an idol between Him and me from now on, but a partner by my side, the way God had ordained it to be. She would be my companion, and together we'd make one whole person. Where I was lacking, she'd fill in the gaps, and vice versa.

I suddenly understood why God discourages divorce; for when a couple separates physically, it doesn't automatically follow that God dissolves the "knot" He tied in the Spirit. I saw that marriage is indeed a mystery. God truly makes a couple into "one flesh." I began to see the beauty of marriage where its headship is found in Christ, with each partner functioning in the God-ordained way: the husband submitting to Christ and the wife submitting to the husband.

When I was finally strong enough to leave the house, Barbara and I attended a prayer meeting where a guest minister had been invited to speak. During the meeting, the minister laid his hands on me and spoke a prophetic message: "You are to be a trumpet. You will warn the people. Your words at times will be very hard on people and they will not like you. But speak the words I give you nevertheless."

When I got home after that meeting, I opened the Bible and Joel 2:1 seemed to jump off the page for me to see: "Blow ye the trumpet . . . for the day of the Lord cometh, for it is nigh at hand."

A few days later, while I was praying, God said to me very emphatically, "Jesus is coming soon. Tell the people!" I was so excited at this revelation that I thought I was the only person in the world who knew it. I made a real effort to get to prayer meetings where I knew people were led of the Holy Spirit—and at every opportunity I'd tell them, "Jesus is coming soon!"

I couldn't understand their lack of enthusiasm when I gave them this message. They seemed so indifferent—and sort of patronizing. "Yes, son, I know," was the usual response. Then they'd look at me a little strangely, furrow their brow, and go on their way. They knew! They all knew! And worse yet, they'd known it for years!

"Listen, Lord!" I stormed when I went home after one such meeting. "Can't you give me bread a little fresher than that?!" I was perturbed and felt pretty foolish to find I was peddling such old news. I felt like a dummy!

It wasn't long, however, before I came to see that many thousands have never heard this message and need to be warned. And the Lord showed me further that Christians who were once excited about the imminent return of Jesus have grown cold and are no longer living lives of expectancy. Maybe this bread was fresher than I realized!

Chapter Seven

THE POT AND THE POTTER

The vessels that I make must not be marred. Therefore, I will keep you on My potting wheel as long as you remain pliable in My hands. But if perchance a pebble be found in you, I can do only one thing: I must stop the work, take the pebble out, and begin anew.*

"Hey, look at this!" Barbara exclaimed, as she yanked my legs up on the edge of the davenport and propped hers next to mine. "Your calf muscles are just as big as mine now!"

"Big deal!" I replied with a grin. "That's not too big, is it?"

"Maybe not," she laughed, "but at least you're not the bag of bones you were a few months ago."

---
* See Jeremiah 18:4.

"Yeah, and I'll tell you something else," I added. "I'm not the bag of *bitterness* I used to be either."

Barbara looked at me thoughtfully. "Bitterness? Wasn't that mentioned to you at the fellowship meeting a few nights ago?"

"Yes. Remember how I was told that God had put His ax to my root of bitterness?"

"Yes, but I'm not sure I understand."

"Well, don't you remember how bitter I became right after I found out I had MS? I resented anyone who was well. I wanted everyone to know what it's like to lose your health, and how hard it is to live captive in a miserable body. I figured I deserved more than that out of life—but God had me cornered."

"But all that bitterness is gone now, isn't it?" Barbara asked confidently.

"Every bit of it. I honestly think I could go through that experience all over again without being so bitter about it."

I was sure that was true. God had been good to me, and I had learned a great deal about trusting Him.

To my own surprise, I was doing a lot of witnessing. The exhilaration of returning health and a better mental outlook was such a blessing that I just couldn't resist telling almost everybody what God had done for me.

But a bolt of lightning struck out of the blue one morning, when I awoke to find the left side of my body weak and trembling. When I tried to stand up, I found that my foot had dropped and I had to pick up my leg with my hands, lift the foot off the floor, and put it down in front for another step.

"Barbara!" I called out woefully. "I've got a problem!"

When she saw me, I noticed a little pool of tears forming in the corner of each eye. I put my arm around her shoulders and tried to comfort her. "It'll be OK," I said. "The Lord's just allowing our faith to be tested. I'll probably be better tomorrow."

But I was no better the next day—nor the next. Weeks began to go by—and still no improvement. I was spending most of my time in bed again—right back where I had started.

"Lord," I said, "what are You doing to me *now?!* All the people I've told about your healing power—now look at me! What a fine mess *I* am, to be telling anybody about victory in Jesus!" It was a puzzling experience.

But though I was confused, I was still inexplainably full of joy. I couldn't understand why I was suffering again, but I had absolutely no bitterness whatsoever. I knew the Lord was in charge, and felt sure He'd bring me through this experience.

Barbara was praying like a house afire those days. She always prayed faithfully, but our circumstances seemed to require some extra petitioning. Yet God seemed to pay no attention. We both felt quite confused—knowing we were called to the ministry on one hand, and being enslaved to sicknesses on the other. It didn't make sense. One morning, however, an answer came.

"I couldn't sleep last night," Barbara said, "so I got up to pray and the Holy Spirit showed me what's going on."

"Come on then," I replied eagerly, sitting up to listen. "Give out with it!"

"I didn't know how to pray for you any more," Barbara told me, "so I just prayed in tongues. I must have prayed about ten minutes when the tongues changed and I started speaking in a language I don't remember ever using before.

"It was a strange experience," she went on. "I knew exactly what I was saying in tongues, and pretty soon I started acting it out as I prayed."

"And what happened?" I was impatient for her to finish.

"You know how a potter sits at a wheel and puts a blob of clay on it?" She waited for my response and I nodded that I was with her so far. "Then he cups his hands around the clay and works it to form whatever he's decided to make as the wheel spins." She looked up at me.

"That's what I was acting out. I was making a vase or something. I sat at a wheel, cupped my hands around the clay and began working it. It was coming along real well, when all of a sudden I raised my hand and smashed the form down into a blob again."

Tears began welling up in her eyes. "Honey," she said softly, "that's what God is doing to you."

My heart sank. "But why? I don't understand."

"Honey, if there is even *one tiny pebble* in a potter's clay, it leaves a mark in the vessel and makes it imperfect. Remember how we talked about God taking the bitterness from you? That was a pebble that God had to take out of you. As long as you had that bitterness, you could never be anything but a marred vessel."

"But that pebble's gone," I protested. "So why is God 'smashing' me again?"

"You never would have known that the pebble was *really* gone if God had not permitted you to go through this one more time. You *said* you could go through it again without getting bitter—but that was only a theory then. But now you know it for sure."

I leaned back against the head of the bed. "Praise the Lord!" I said with bated breath. "I think you've found the answer!"

"Yes, and the best part is, God's starting all over again to make a really beautiful vessel."

"Yeah," I replied, "and let's hope He doesn't find any more pebbles in my clay!"

Several days after that revelation, God spoke to me about my sickness. "Go to a Kathryn Kuhlman service. She will lay her hands on you and pray for you, and you will be healed!"

Ridiculous! I argued with myself and Barbara that that could not have been from God. I knew the Scriptures about healing—especially that we were healed by the stripes Jesus bore on his back (1 Peter 2:24 and Isaiah 53:5) and that God promised to heal all our diseases (Psalm 103:3). But previously, God had healed me at home without an intermediary. I knew perfectly well that He could heal me at home again.

Besides, Kathryn Kuhlman doesn't usually have prayer lines and lay hands on the sick. Rather, miraculous healings take place out in the audience while she is preaching—and she tells people not to come up front until they've been healed. Thousands attend her meetings, and I doubted seriously that I could even get near her. What made me think she would lay hands on me and pray for me? But I wasn't getting any better. So what else was there to do?

I dreaded the trip. It was a nine-hour drive from our house to the First Presbyterian Church in Pittsburgh, where Miss Kuhlman held her services. We'd have to be there by six o'clock in the morning, if not earlier, to get close enough to have half a chance of getting in the doors. The doors would be opened at 9:00, but the service wouldn't begin until around ten, and we'd have to sit there until it was over in the early afternoon. I just wasn't anxious to put myself through all that; but I had read in the Bible that obedience is better than sacrifice,* so I decided I'd better go.

We started for Pittsburgh on a Thursday morning. The trip was exhausting—and when we arrived at the motel where we'd planned to spend the night, we found that they didn't have a room near the parking lot. Instead, they gave us a suite in the inner court. I had to maneuver myself up steps and down a long path to reach the room. I'd rather have slept in the driveway!

At six in the morning, we were part of a crowd of people sitting on the front steps of the church—but we were close enough to the doors so that we knew we'd get in.

When eight o'clock came, I found out what the

---
* 1 Samuel 15:22.

Bible means where it records that the crowds *pressed* to see Jesus. If I had taken both feet off the ground, I would still have been held upright by the people pushing toward the door in their anxiety not to be left out.

When the doors finally did open, Barbara made her way down the main floor as far to the front as she could find seats, and waited for me to be carried along by the crowd. Finally I joined her and we sat together and waited. The music started by ten, and when Miss Kuhlman came in wearing her white pulpit dress, I pulled myself to my feet along with the thousands of others present. How I enjoyed seeing this woman receive a standing ovation! It did my heart good to see her get the respect she so richly deserves.

The huge congregation filled the main floor, the balcony, the anterooms, the basement—and hundreds were locked outside because there was no more room inside. Miss Kuhlman asked all of us to lift our faces toward heaven (that's the way Jesus prayed), and to begin reverently singing praises.

Soon the Holy Spirit began to move upon the congregation, and one could hear sobs of gratitude all over the large church as people received healing. As usual, however, Miss Kuhlman did not go to the people, nor lay hands on any and pray for them, as God had said she would do for me. With so many thousands there, it seemed unlikely that such a thing could happen.

By two o'clock the service was nearly over, although the air still seemed charged as if with electricity. People were quietly crying for joy all over the building. But nothing had happened to me. I was beginning to feel that God had really let me down.

But suddenly Miss Kuhlman left the pulpit. She walked down the aisle and stopped at the row where Barbara and I were sitting. Her eyes scanned the whole row; then, motioning with her very expressive hands, she encouraged the whole row, "Come out; God wants to touch you."

Everyone in our row stood and walked out into the aisle. Barbara and I were near the end. Miss Kuhlman touched each one lightly on the face; as the power of the Holy Spirit went through their bodies, they fell to the floor. It reminded me of what happened to the Apostle Paul and those with him when he was on the road to Damascus and saw a vision of Christ (Acts 26:14). It didn't matter if a man were six and a half feet tall, and weighed three hundred pounds—down he'd go.

But when she prayed for Barbara and me, nothing happened. All the others were lying on the floor, basking in the glory of God—but we just stood there like disappointed statues.

Miss Kuhlman went back to the pulpit, while Barbara and I stepped over the prostrate bodies and worked our way back into the pew. I was thinking, "Well, anyway, she laid hands on me; maybe that's what God meant."

Just as Barbara and I were sitting down, I glanced up to see that Miss Kuhlman had turned around and was coming back in our direction, as though she had forgotten something. She came directly to Barbara.

Laying a hand on Barbara's cheek, she said, "Someone very close to you is suffering with a nerve condition."

"That's me," I interrupted.

"Ah," she sighed, a big smile breaking over her face. Laying her hands on my shoulders, she said with authority, "I rebuke this nerve condition in the name of Jesus!"

Again nothing happened. The Holy Spirit did not knock me on the floor. There was no warm feeling or sensation of electricity like other people said they felt when they were healed. Nothing—absolutely nothing happened. But she *had* laid her hands on me and prayed for me! Isn't that what God said would happen?

After the service, Barbara helped me drag myself out of the church and we made the long drive back to Hartford almost in silence. Once home, I collapsed in bed, thoroughly discouraged.

The next morning, I awakened with my left side completely healed!

The problem was gone, and I could walk normally. I felt so good, I could hardly believe it was me!

"Barbara!" I shouted. "Look at me! I'm healed!"

When she came into the bedroom and saw me, she threw her arms around me and we almost danced for joy, praising and thanking God for another miracle.

Later, when I asked Him why I hadn't been healed in Miss Kuhlman's service, a gentle Voice within replied, "You wanted to be healed at home so badly, I waited until you got here!" I couldn't help but laugh delightedly at the Lord's colorfulness—but I didn't miss what He was trying to tell me about obedience. Had I not gone to the Kuhlman meeting as God had instructed, I might not have received the healing. I saw that obedience to the Lord is a weighty matter.

I recalled a story in First Kings 20 about a certain man who lost his very life because he hadn't obeyed a "thus saith the Lord." Apparently the command had seemed unreasonable, and the man had simply refused to obey. Imagine how shocked he must have been, then, when the prophet of God said to him, "Because thou hast not obeyed the voice of the Lord, behold, as soon as thou art departed from me, a lion shall slay thee" (1 Kings 20:36).

If the man was tempted to scoff at this prophecy, he quickly became a believer when, a few minutes later, a lion pounced on him. But too late. In a matter of minutes, it was all over.

Not that God would have slain me for disobedience —but I was thankful that I hadn't foolishly taken the chance of sacrificing my leg by not obeying the command to go to Pittsburgh.

Even after that miracle, though, I was not sufficiently convalesced to permit my going back to work. Apparently, He still had something more to teach me while I sat at home alone all day.

Some days I'd get the "housewife blues." I didn't like being cooped up in the house all day, and I looked forward to short rides in the car when Barbara came home in the evening. It seemed that a cloud of depression hung over me.

My hours of sleeping and waking were almost completely reversed. If Barbara awoke at night, she'd find me reading the Bible or in prayer. Between one and four o'clock in the morning, my vision became so sharp that I could read the smallest print without glasses; during the day my vision was such that I could read only larger print. My ophthalmologist couldn't explain this phenomenon, so I assumed it was God giving me that time especially to learn about Him through His Word.

About that time, we "happened" to attend a fellowship meeting where we heard a teaching on warfare against Satan and his demons. That night, for the first time, we saw people delivered of demon spirits in the name of Jesus. We had not realized until that night that about one-fourth of Jesus' ministry on earth was devoted to delivering those oppressed by demons.

We were shown that we do not wrestle "against flesh and blood, but against principalities, against powers, against the rulers of the darkness of this world" (Ephesians 6:12). When we feel depressed and disgruntled, we wrongly try to put the blame on everything and everybody except Satan and his demons; this is just one of his tricks, for he doesn't want us to recognize him; he'd rather exercise his authority unrecognized and unchallenged.

It was pointed out that demon spirits are not part of our carnal nature. The Bible teaches us to *crucify* the carnal nature, but to *cast out* demon spirits. If there is something ugly in one's life which will not die—which will not succumb to crucifixion, prayer, and discipline—it could be a demon spirit. And the only way it can be dealt with, we were told, is by casting it out. We saw that Christians do come under demonic attack, and that demons continually seek to influence certain areas of a Christian's life. But we don't need to put up with this oppression, we were told. These demons can be cast out in the name of Jesus.

By the time the teaching was over that night, I realized why I was having such a continual struggle with depression. I had become the target of a spirit of depression when I was blind, and had carried it around for three years. Some depression would have been normal under the circumstances, but Satan had taken advantage. Unknowingly, I had given in to this evil spirit while I cowered like an animal in my hospital bed. And ever since that time, I had been plagued with extreme moodiness and depression, even after my healing.

Asking for prayer that night, I was amazed when I actually *felt* this depressing spirit rise up in my chest, and was able to cough it out.

One more pebble gone! But still God wasn't done with me.

Chapter Eight

SACKCLOTH AND ASHES

"Though you exalt yourself as the eagle, and though you set your nest among the stars, thence will I bring you down...." *

I thought the day of recuperation would never end. But eventually God began to stir up my spirit, and I felt impressed to go away for a week on a private retreat to fast and pray for further direction. As a result I was led to buy an organ. Our savings were gone, and we owed hundreds upon hundreds of dollars to the hospital, even after insurance coverage. Certainly we could not afford such a luxury—but God evidently wanted us to have it, because the money came in from a totally unexpected source. We

---
* Obadiah 3, paraphrased.

were given $850.00 in one lump sum—and the organ God told us to buy cost $849.52!

Neither Barbara nor I was a musician. A few months earlier, however, someone in one of the fellowship meetings we attended had prophesied to Barbara that God was going to give her a ministry in song. Barbara had already done a little singing in a very amateurish way—but from that time on, she noticed something different. Whenever she was asked to sing, something about the size of a ping-pong ball would form in her throat, and she would sound like a trained singer.

When this had first happened, we'd both been startled. When she was under this anointing, people would weep, and later on a few even reported being healed while she sang. It was as if her voice "plowed" the way for God's seed to be planted in people's hearts in the preaching that followed.

I soon learned to pick out melodies on the organ with my right hand, while chording with my left. Though my accompaniment left much to be desired, I was at least able to help Barbara practice a few songs. For one solid year, we put songs together and I practiced sermons. It was discouraging, though, because there was no goal to work toward. We had no ministry, and Barbara wasn't getting any invitations to sing. But God had given Barbara a talent, and she felt she had to do her part by preparing herself so that He could use her when He wanted to.

Whenever someone asked her to sing for the sake of entertainment rather than ministry, it never sounded quite the same. The effect just wasn't there. Her voice was only for the purpose of glorifying God and preparing people to receive the ministry of the Word.

God never did give me a talent for accompanying her in public. That was not my calling. But He did use me to help her get started at home. I accompanied her as best I could, and encouraged her to keep trying when she became frustrated and discouraged.

So there we were: Barbara singing and me preaching to living room furniture for a whole year, with no plans in mind. We were just practicing because the Holy Spirit had led us to do it—and we sometimes felt a little foolish about the whole thing. I had always said I would *never* be a preacher, but God was changing my heart and giving me the desire to preach.

A year of practicing can be an awfully long time. Perhaps it wouldn't have been necessary to wait that long if I'd been listening to God carefully enough. I guess I just became so accustomed to the routine of practicing that I didn't ask God earnestly enough what we were practicing *for!*

But God knew how to force me to my knees and get my full attention. I'd gone to the doctor a week earlier for my flu shot, and, wouldn't you know it, I came down with one wallopaloozer of a case of the flu right after. I was so sick that I wanted to die.

When my wife called the doctor, his unconsoling response was, "There's nothing I can do, Mrs. Foley. These things happen with multiple sclerosis. There's nothing anybody can do about it. You'll have to wait it out and hope for the best."

I couldn't believe it. The flu was diagnosed as MS. It was apparent that the label "diseased" was on me, and it wouldn't matter any more if I had an ingrown toenail, it would be blamed on MS.

The flu was a terrible shock to my system—and a few days later, another complication set in (which seems to be the story of my life): my eyes froze in their sockets. I couldn't move them left, right, up, or down. I could only look directly forward or turn my whole head to see anything that wasn't straight ahead. About that time I realized I'd better start to do a little more praying—which was exactly what God wanted.

It wasn't long before the healing came. The flu left and my eyes loosened again. On the heels of the healing came the word God had wanted to give me: that Barbara and I were to form an association through which we could promote the Gospel.

"What are we going to call it, Barbara?" I asked her one morning over bacon and eggs.

"Well," Barbara replied, "God called you to be a 'trumpet'—and, from what we read last night in the Bible, we know a trumpet was used to call people to arms, and to warn them or gather them together for some important event. What event could be more important than the return of the Lord Jesus? How about *Trumpeteers?*"

"That's it!" I exploded. "We'll call it 'The Trumpeteers Evangelistic Association.' How's that sound?"

"Fine," she said. "I like the idea of calling it an *evangelistic* association. You'd never make a pastor, but 'evangelist'—that does suit your character and seems right in the Lord."

I sent a dollar to the state capital for a book on corporate law. A few months later, after much study of that book and much prayer for guidance from the Holy Spirit, I became the founder of "The Trumpeteers Evangelistic Association, Inc."

On August 3, 1970, Barbara and I announced our organization to a mailing list of 120 people. Then we sat back to wait for invitations. In essence, we were telling the public, "Here we are, folks, all ready to serve you. Now just take advantage of this great opportunity!"

What a rude awakening when no one responded! All of August went by with no invitations. September came and went—still no response. Halfway through October, I was becoming quite anxious. I knew God had called me into the ministry—so where were the invitations? It took a while before I began to realize that God wasn't about to use me until I had met a couple more requirements besides being saved and baptized in the Holy Spirit!

While I was doing my best to live a righteous life, and was saying to the Lord, "Here am I; send me"— yet, like Isaiah, I needed a special cleansing—a cleansing that would make me a fit servant for the Lord.

The impression came strongly that I was to spend *one month* away from home at a Bible school in New York where I knew the emphasis was very heavy on prophetic teaching. I thought the Lord was sending me there to give me a better understanding of these things in order that I might teach them to others. And, with that in mind, off I went.

But I learned a lot more than prophecy during that

month! In a far more intense way, the Holy Spirit cleaned me up, convicted me of heretofore unrecognized sins, changed my attitudes, and showed me the importance of personal holiness.

When the month was up and I came home, Barbara said, "I can't get over how you've changed!"

"Is that good or bad?" I asked.

"Oh, that's good," she said. "I've been praying for it a long time."

But still no invitations came, though we waited and waited. Finally, the Lord sent a man of God to my door—a man I have come to love in the Lord because of his beautiful prophetic ministry. On that day, he, Barbara and I sat at the kitchen table and the Word of the Lord was opened to me. We read and discussed the third chapter of First Timothy, where ministerial duties are explained. After we studied and prayed together, I was charged to carry out the duties of a minister. Then our friend took oil and anointed me for the ministry—not merely with a dab on my forehead, but in the same way the Bible describes the anointing of Aaron: ". . . like the precious ointment upon the head, that ran down upon the beard . . . that went down to the skirts of his garments" (Psalm 133:2). Oil was poured all over me—and as it flowed, I felt the Spirit of the Lord anointing me with power. I was sure this day marked something special in the Spirit.

With that accomplished, invitations began coming in. Doors that would not open previously now swung wide—and I saw that God had been holding me back until I had been anointed, cleansed, and separated to the ministry. One pastor invited Barbara and me to minister at his church for one Sunday evening a month throughout that winter and into the following spring. The Lord must have done a great work of grace in those people, judging by the way they put up with us all that time! I don't say that lightly. Most of the parishioners were established in the Lord—certainly more so than either Barbara or I.

We had practically nothing to give them. But the Lord had to teach us how to stand in front of people somewhere—and He picked that church. We were so unpolished! I was still under the impression that a preacher had to yell, or his message wouldn't get through. I would stand behind the pulpit, ranting and raving, piercing tender eardrums with my shrill voice, making children plug up their ears with their fingers.

Occasionally, though, the Lord helped someone through our ministry—probably to encourage the congregation to keep on putting up with me until I got over my stage fright.

It seemed to me that God was teaching me how to deal with others, and it gave me a good feeling when I saw myself improving. I was getting to be quite a big shot!

I'll never forget the way God dealt with my pride. I knew it had to come. God had talked to me all too many times about that. How could he ever use me with all this conceit in my heart? I was greatly troubled about it as I went to bed one night—but I didn't know how to deal with it.

At 5:00 A.M., I was startled awake by an audible Voice.

"Repent in sacksloth and ashes!" the Voice commanded.

I sat bolt upright in bed and looked around in the semidarkness. No one was there except Barbara, who was sleeping peacefully at my side.

Was that God speaking? I couldn't imagine why God would say such a strange thing. I knew from my Bible reading that God often called on people in Old Testament times to wear sackcloth and ashes as a sign of repentance and humility—but surely not in these times!

Two days later Barbara and I were riding home from a trip we had taken. I hadn't told her about the strange message. Just as we were nearing home, I thought, "I'm going to see if this is really You, Lord. If Barbara wants to stop at the fruit stand before we get home without my suggesting it, I'll inquire there about sackcloth."

I knew my wife's habits pretty well. She always went right home after a trip. If she needed anything, she'd drop me off at home and go to the store later. So I felt quite sure we wouldn't be stopping *anywhere*.

Imagine my surprise, then, when Barbara pulled up to the fruit stand and said, "Honey, I could really go for some apple cider. See if they have any, will you?" I felt my heart beating a little faster.

After I'd picked up the jug of cider, I asked the clerk if he had any burlap sacks he was going to throw out. I figured burlap was the same as sackcloth, and I knew potatoes were sometimes delivered in such sacks. But he said he'd just thrown them all out that morning. I couldn't help saying "Hallelujah" under my breath!

After ringing up my purchase on the register and taking my money, the clerk put the jug in a large paper bag, thanked me politely and headed for a back room. I put my change in my pocket, and was about to pick up my bag and walk out when I heard the clerk calling to me, "Hey, mister, I found one. There was a sack on the floor in the back corner. I don't know how it was missed, but you can have it."

"Thanks," I muttered, taking it from him. I stuffed it into the paper bag with the cider and walked to the car, hoping Barbara wouldn't see it and start asking questions.

"OK, Lord," I said when we got home. "What about ashes? I don't have any around here."

"Yes, you do," came the little Voice within. "In the hibachi outside on the back porch." Sure enough. I had forgotten we even had a hibachi. We hadn't used it for a good year, but it was still full of ashes from the previous summer.

I waited nervously until Barbara was sound asleep that night. Then, easing myself out of bed about 2 A.M., I sneaked out to the back porch to get the little hibachi. Once I was back in the kitchen, I turned on a light and pulled out the burlap sack from the place where I'd hidden it. Removing my night clothes, I wrapped the scratchy burlap around my hips and sat in the middle of the kitchen floor to pray.

I felt ridiculous. Who, in his right mind, would do a thing like this? I just hoped that Barbara wouldn't wake up and find me in this outfit!

Not knowing for certain what God wanted me to do next, I prayed in tongues for a while. Then I pulled the hibachi closer and took a handful of ashes. I had looked up a number of Scripture references in preparation for this "night of humiliation," and I knew that the prophets who girded themselves in sackcloth usually threw ashes all over themselves. So I began to sprinkle the ashes on my arms, praying in tongues at the same time.

As I prayed, I began speaking in a language I'd never used before—one that sounded completely different from the tongue the Holy Spirit usually gave me. The utterance was very brief—and then, in a flash, I received the interpretation, the Holy Spirit speaking to me quietly through my own lips.

"Throw the ashes all over thyself," the Spirit said.

I obeyed, throwing the ashes on my chest, back and legs, and tossing some into the air to settle on my face. What a mess! Ashes were in my hair. They were all over me. I choked on the dust. I felt grimy, grubby, and stupid—but I was getting excited about the message that was coming.

"Rub it in," the Spirit urged. "Rub it in. All over. Rub it in."

I followed the instructions, rubbing myself until my face and all of my body were black with sooty ashes.

"Now see thyself," the Lord said. There was a pause that I might have a moment to look at my dirty arms, legs, and body. Then He said, "Thou art just as filthy inside as thou art outside!"

A sickish, empty feeling engulfed me, and I began to weep. I had tried so hard to live a clean life—and now God was telling me I was still this filthy! I was overcome with a sense of worthlessness and helplessness to do any better.

After about half an hour, I regained my composure enough to pray again, and once more the Spirit spoke: "My son, go and wash thyself."

As I showered, I began to understand the Apostle Paul. He wasn't merely being humble when he said, "In me . . . dwelleth no good thing" (Romans 7:18). He wasn't speaking in false humility. He knew the fact of it. He had the revelation on it. The Prophet Isaiah knew the fact of it, too. He asserted, "All our righteousnesses are as filthy rags" (Isaiah 64:6).

God certainly has ways of making His Word come alive to our hearts. In that moment I knew that *only Jesus is pure*. The only way we can be clean is to have Jesus living in us. It's His righteousness that we get through on, certainly not our own.

That was a shattering, humbling experience for me. God brought my soul into humility, and never again would I exalt myself in my own mind. Never again would I think that, apart from Him, I could do anything worthy of His praise.

Chapter Nine

NO SILVER-TONGUED ORATOR

Do not complicate your walk with Me with nonessential considerations. For what do I require of you, but "to do justly, and to love mercy, and to walk humbly" with Me? *

Lest I give in to the pride of saying I was finally humble, God began taking me through a number of experiences designed to *keep* me humble (and believe me, I must have aggravated His patience in accomplishing this!)

I was invited to a rather reserved New England church for an Ash Wednesday service, oddly enough. (I was tempted to take my hibachi!) Our ministry was becoming a little more fruitful by that time and I was beginning to follow the Holy Spirit more care-

---
* Micah 6:8.

fully—if one can learn how to follow the wind! That's how unpredictable the Holy Spirit often seems. My preaching had even become a little less noisy, I thought.

The service was going fairly well, although I could sense some degree of spiritual apathy in that church. The people were *hearing* the Gospel, but it wasn't registering. I could feel that. They weren't free in Jesus, and I was trying so hard to get them to see His light.

Right in the middle of my sermon a woman popped up and said loudly, "Mr. Foley, I'm sorry, but you're making me very angry—and you're hurting my ears!"

The Lord must have had control of me in that moment; otherwise, at that point in my spiritual growth, I would have wanted to punch her in the face. If she thought it was easy to get a point through to a group of sober-faced, unresponsive pew-warmers, she had another thought coming!

But the Holy Spirit, with His quiet peace, began to flood over me. To my surprise, I said to the woman, "I'm sorry if I've offended you—but I can't apologize for the Gospel I'm preaching. It's God's Word and it's Truth. If you'd rather, perhaps you'd like to sit farther back."

She seemed grateful for the suggestion and was quick to move to the back of the sanctuary. I picked up my message in a milder tone and began where I'd left off.

At the end of the message, I gave an altar call, and the woman's husband was the first to respond. In tears, he literally ran down the aisle, and about fourteen others followed him. I don't think I've ever witnessed such eagerness to come to Jesus as I witnessed in that old church that night. Many members were weeping openly, and a strong spirit of repentance was evident. In His perfect way, God had used that woman to keep me humble and, at the same time, had kept me composed enough to see the service through to victory.

Invitations to minister continued to come in. One day, however, I received a *special* invitation—a really important one. It was an invitation to speak at a Full Gospel Businessmen's breakfast.

For some reason, I was just positive that if I blew this appearance, it would mean the end of my ministry. So I began to prepare early. I ordered dozens of sermon records by famous fundamentalist preachers and listened to them for weeks before the engagement. There was one in particular that I liked, and I listened to it until I had it just about memorized. I certainly didn't consider myself expert enough to be able to write my own sermon for such an important occasion as this one. But I didn't see how I could miss if I used a great sermon like this.

I practiced preaching the sermon every day while Barbara was at work, trying to make sure I knew exactly how to say everything just like the speaker on the record. When I had it down pat, I invited my wife to sit in for a dry run.

She sat on the couch and listened attentively. I went through the whole thing as if it were for real, giving it everything I had.

"What do you think?" I asked proudly when I finished. I thought I'd done a great job.

God heard that—and surely must have inspired Barbara to say just the right thing to keep me from further vanity.

"That's not you," she said as lovingly as she could, knowing how hard I must have worked. But no amount of sweetness was going to soften the sting of those words.

"Honey," she said, "you don't talk like that. You have plenty to say. Why don't you say things your own way? Be what you are instead of trying to fit into somebody else's shoes. You're trying to talk like a silver-tongued orator, and you're just not that."

I was deflated. Leave it to a wife to say it like it is! It had taken me a month to prepare that sermon. I was too nervous to talk off the top of my head like a professional speaker. The breakfast was now only three days away. How could I possibly get anything together now?

The next day, all I could do was pace back and forth. I was like a baby bird who had just been issued "flying papers" by his mother. I was sure I was going to fall flat on my beak! I was nervous, angry that I hadn't received approval, and excited all at the same time.

But when I finally became quiet before the Lord, I heard Him say to me, "Depend on Me. Relax." Soon a few verses from the Bible popped into my mind along with some ideas for the sermon.

I worked over these ideas, but never did get them down on paper the way I wanted them. All too soon, the Saturday morning of the breakfast arrived, and Barbara drove me to the restaurant where the meeting was to be held. I felt like I was being driven to my own funeral.

My stomach was too squeamish to accept any food. I kept a glass of water handy, however, to keep my lips from sticking to my teeth—a symptom of nervous dry-mouth.

Even though it was a blustery winter morning, there were over a hundred people present. When the people finished eating, Barbara began the program with a few songs, "plowing the way" for me to plant the seeds of the Gospel. My message was based on Romans 13:11-14. It was all about waking up to the times we're living in, and understanding the nearness of the Lord's return. I also explained how to get ready for the Great Event.

In spite of my shakiness, the Lord anointed the message and there was a long prayer line when I gave the invitation afterward. Many were healed, saved, and baptized in the Holy Spirit.

The meeting was a real "shot in the arm" for me and an unforgettable lesson about trusting the Lord to give me the message needed by the people to whom I'm called upon to minister at a particular place and time. He made it clear that I wasn't to preach stale messages which had long since lost their anointing. He reminded me that I could draw from rivers of living water, rather than resorting to old cistern water. If I'd stay in tune with the Spirit every day—not just when I'm preparing for a service—He would give me messages that were fresh and needful.

"Lord," I said later, "I think I'm finally learning to depend on You for everything—including a good supply of humility!"

There were times, however, when I would get to feeling a little sorry for myself. I wondered if others experienced the same sort of humiliations which had become so common in my life. It seemed that my pride was forever being punched down—but I knew there was no other way for God to make me usable, and I *did* want to be used. But it surprised me when I discovered how He used my bumbling efforts to break pride in another.

Barbara and I had been invited by Pastor Hugh Smith to minister at his church in Williamstown, Vermont. At this particular meeting, Barbara sang and I gave my personal testimony, along with a short, unimpressive message. At least, I *thought* it was unimpressive. But when I came down from the platform to pray for the people's needs, I sensed immediately that the Holy Spirit was there to heal. It was like a page out of the book of Acts. Arms and legs were lengthened. People were delivered from chronic back ailments, demon oppression, skin diseases, migraine headaches—and the pastor's wife was healed of severe hypoglycemia. The altar was five deep with people giving their hearts to Jesus. Of course, Barbara and I were jubilant as we traveled home, but we had no idea then how this powerful meeting had shaken Hugh Smith.

He told us all about it later. During the service he began experiencing a "suffocating force" pressing in around him. As he sat there in the pew, he began to realize that he had been living a lie. He felt that his mind had become diseased with pride and that he had become guilty of the very thing he had condemned in others: having a form of godliness, but denying the power thereof. After attending a seminary where intellectualism was the "god of the campus," his mind had become clouded with questions about the identity of Jesus, doubts about the practicality of what He said, and skepticism about his ability to do anything miraculous today. A professional preacher whose life had gone to pot, his chief delight was the composition and delivery of admirable sermons. He confessed that he had millions of excuses why he could not take time to be alone with the Lord, learn how to walk in the Spirit, and teach his people about God's power. By the time we had our service in his church, his heart was heavy with guilt, pride and rebellion. He felt physically exhausted, emotionally drained, and spiritually bankrupt.

The day after our service, Hugh boarded a plane alone and went in search of help from some friends who had earlier introduced him to the reality of the Holy Spirit. When he arrived, he was greeted by them with open arms and soon found himself preaching in their church. Though he tried to deliver a decent sermon, he wasn't able to contain the spiritual brokenness he felt.

"I cried like a baby," he confessed, "and was it ever humiliating!" He said he hadn't been able to cry in years—not even privately—but there he was exposing his burdened heart between heavy sobbing and pauses to compose himself!

God saw those tears. The love of the Lord was poured out on Hugh and, in his brokenness, he was able to receive it.

Within moments, Hugh found himself surrounded by compassionate friends. A message in tongues was given by one of the men praying for him, followed by the interpretation: "I am the only Way, Truth and Life. Yield to Me. Take My hand and I will lead you."

Hugh later had the opportunity to explain to his parishioners how God had dealt with him. Some understood—but others did not. Some of them thought he'd had a nervous breakdown and needed to be dismissed.

He told me later, "They didn't understand that the only thing that had been broken was my pride—not my nerves!"

Maybe *they* didn't understand but *I* did!

Chapter Ten

HUMS, BUZZES AND UH-OHS

Before honor is humility." [*] *This is what I would have you learn in every circumstance. You must go down before you go up. First the breaking, then the building. First the trouble, then the triumph.*

I was excited, yet somewhat apprehensive, the day Barbara and I began to talk seriously about making her first singing album. I always felt "up-tight" when I saw large debts looming before me—and we'd found out from Baldwin Sound Productions that we'd need nearly three thousand dollars to produce the record. The first thousand would be due when the contract was signed; the second thousand, at recording time; and the balance when the albums were delivered.

----
[*] Proverbs 15:33.

Mulling it over and over in my mind, I said to Barbara, "Where in the world are we going to get three thousand dollars?"

"Oh, honey!" she laughed. "Where is all that faith you're supposed to have?"

"OK," I said sarcastically, "I'll go right out and pick it off our money tree."

But I saw that Barbara was right. If God wanted us to make this album, He'd provide the money, wouldn't He? And sure enough, He did. From here and there, gifts of money were given—and after a lot of scraping and saving, we got the first thousand together by the day before the contract-signing. Trusting that God would provide the remainder when it was needed, we put our signatures on the agreement and walked out of the Baldwin offices realizing what a "ridiculous" thing we'd just done.

But God came through. He supplied not only the second thousand before the actual recording date, but the entire balance by then, too!

The album, entitled *Make a Joyful Noise unto the Lord*, was released in 1971. It was a beautiful album and carried a stunning picture of Barbara on the jacket. There was one small problem, though. We had decided to use Barbara's first and middle names —Barbara Carol—instead of the first and last— Barbara Foley. "Barbara Carol" had a nice ring to it, we thought.

But then the misunderstandings began. Some people who didn't know us thought Barbara's *last* name was Carol. I'd receive mail addressed to "Barbara Carol and husband." Sometimes I'd answer the telephone and be asked if I were Mr. Carol. When I said, "No, I'm Mr. *Foley*," that only made matters worse—for then they'd wonder what Mr. Foley was doing living with Barbara Carol! One fellow supposed that I was Barbara's agent, but he later told me he wondered why a Christian singer would be living with her agent. Some people even suspected that we had a common-law marriage. Talk about humiliation!

In spite of all this confusion, God blessed the album, and they sold so quickly that about a year later we decided to produce a second one titled *I'm So Happy!* That helped open the way for Barbara's ministry, and she received a number of invitations to speak and/or sing at various women's functions. As I prayed about our ministry, God promised us greater things to come.

After a while, I began to think about the possibility of a weekly radio ministry. I could use selections from Barbara's albums, and could follow them by preaching, teaching, interviewing guests, or whatever God led me to do.

One day I said to Barbara, "What would you think about putting our ministry on the radio? We could call our program 'The Trumpet Sound.'"

"That would be great!" Barbara replied enthusiastically. "Radio is an important medium, and I should think God would have us take advantage of it."

"Well, let's look into it," I suggested. "It might be beyond our means right now, but I'll call a few stations and find out what the rates are."

The result of those calls was that we signed contracts with three different stations in Connecticut—

and we didn't have the slightest idea about how to produce a radio broadcast!

In the first place, we needed equipment. We thought the program ought to be tape-recorded, but to do it right we needed another recorder besides the one we already had. We began to pray for God to supply this need. In a short time, I came across one that I thought would fill the bill. But I felt God telling me to wait a month and I would get it at the wholesale price. The $350 retail price was beyond our reach.

I did return in a month and, sure enough, because it was the only one left, the store manager sold it to me for the wholesale price of $260.

Now the problem was where to put the equipment. Our home was small, but we didn't know of any other place where we could produce our broadcasts—so, out went the dining room, and in came the recording studio.

The complications were endless. Special cords that I needed couldn't be found, so I had to make my own. Plugs that were supposed to fit into certain places didn't. Buttons that were supposed to make the recorders work didn't respond to my touch.

Finally, though, I surmounted all these problems and began my first experimental recording. After a few minutes of "speaking into the mike," I rewound the tape to listen. All I could hear was a great big hum, with a voice resembling mine somewhere in the distance. I traced the problem to a faulty connection and fixed that.

It took me four hours to make the first fifteen-minute program. I didn't know how to go about getting Barbara's songs from the albums to my tapes. I finally tried putting the record on our stereo and picking up the music through the microphone. Once I had the song on tape, I cut out that segment of tape and spliced it into my program with splicing tape. Then I did my preaching, which was supposed to take up the rest of the time, but didn't—so I kept on talking about something or other until the time was up.

When I played back the first tape, it sounded tinny. Not knowing what to do about it, I decided to let it go. My deadline dates were drawing near, and I needed to produce something—almost anything! I had decided that I ought to do programs for a quarter of a year (thirteen weeks) in one giant recording session. But the session was even longer than I expected. It took me six weeks to make the programs on a master tape and to run copies for each of the three stations. After I had them all made, it never occurred to me that I ought to check them over before sending them to the radio stations. That would have taken hours, and the flower of patience in my life wasn't exactly in full bloom.

Barbara and I waited nervously for the first Sunday morning broadcast over the local station—then suddenly, "The Trumpet Sound" was on the air!

But something was wrong. The music still sounded tinny and muffled. I knew immediately that I had made a mistake in trying to pick up the singing with the microphone. I should have run a line directly into the recorder. I was painfully embarrassed, but I couldn't do all those tapes over, could I? I talked myself into believing that it didn't sound all *that* bad. I would just forget it this time and make sure I did the next batch of tapes right.

On Monday, I received a telephone call from the manager of one of our stations seventy miles away.

"You'll have to check over your tapes," the man said. "I think you've got trouble."

"Why? What's wrong with them?" I asked in a worried tone of voice.

"Well, on yesterday's program you had two tracks playing at the same time. It sounded like a bunch of gobbledygook. You must have forgotten to erase that particular tape before you started recording."

"Dum-dee-dum-dum!" I groaned under my breath —then exploded with, "You didn't let *that* go out over the air for fifteen minutes, I hope!"

"Why, sure we did!" he replied. "You paid for the time and that's what you sent us—so what was I to do?"

I felt like tearing my hair out. After all my hard work to put those tapes on the air on time, all I got for it was nowhere and embarrassment.

I realized that the gobbledygook tape might not be the only one like it. And even if the other tapes weren't like that, the singing segments just weren't up to par. I decided I'd better do something.

So I rigged up a line and started in to do twelve programs all over again. By working sixteen hours a day, I finished them in two weeks, and made the rounds to the studios to replace the first programs with the new ones. By the time I got back home, I thought I would collapse from nervous exhaustion.

"The Trumpet Sound" radio ministry certainly had a struggling beginning—so much so that I began to wonder after a time if it had really been the Lord telling me to put the programs on the air; maybe it was, after all, only another upsurge of fleshly pride that made me think I could undertake such a difficult and expensive endeavor as a radio ministry. Satan began to tell me that I really didn't have much to say. Others could teach and preach so much better than I. Let them be on the air. Besides, the cost of air time seemed to be getting out of hand with programs on three stations.

So, one day, I decided to discontinue the program on one of the stations. I told myself that I could handle two stations better than three. I tried desperately to look at my decision as correcting an error, all the time fighting off thoughts that I was going backward instead of forward in the ministry. I called the station manager and told him of my decision. Then I just put it out of my mind.

A few days later, however, he called me back. "We announced that your program is going off the air," he said. "But I think you should know that we've received a goodly number of calls from listeners asking us to please continue it. They thought it was *our* decision to cancel it. Doug, are you sure you want to take it off? Tell you what. I'll give you half price for air time if you'll stay with us!"

"Half price, huh? That sounds pretty good," I said. "But I still don't know. Even *that's* a big bite—and besides, I'm not too thrilled with the time slot you've given me. Everybody's sleeping then."

"What time do you want?" the manager asked.

"I'd prefer somewhere around 10:00 A.M.," I told him frankly.

"It's yours!" he said.

"Well, let me check with my associates," I replied. "I'll call you back shortly." And I hung up the receiver.

The "associates" I had in mind were God and my wife. But before I had a chance to ask God or talk with Barbara, the Holy Spirit gave me such a mighty outpouring of joy and peace that I *knew* beyond any doubt that God wanted me to accept the station manager's offer. But even more important. I *knew* God wanted me in radio.

All this time I'd been going along by faith, believing God was making our radio ministry possible, but never having complete assurance that I was in His will until I tried to back out. Now He wouldn't *let* me back out! (That seems to be one of the Lord's favorite ways of dealing with me. He makes me move out on faith, and I find myself trusting and hoping I'm following the right course. Then, *after* I've stepped out, He confirms His will to me. It would be easier to walk by sight, but that's not God's way.)

God broadened our outreach as we sent out quarterly messages to a growing mailing list, provided a Bible Study Course, and began a tape ministry. One thing became very clear, though—that in every circumstance, God was keeping the *old* Doug Foley right where he belonged.

Learning to depend on God completely wasn't easy for me. My old, proud, self-sufficient nature wanted to scheme and plan and raise money for our growing expenses. I didn't see how we'd make it on faith, especially when Barbara quit her job and came into the ministry full time, and the cost of living was soaring. I had to fight to remind myself: *God is my source. I must trust Him.*

Then God reminded me of the day a few years earlier when He had shown me how much He cares. I had spent most of the day pacing the floor, worrying about our bills. When Barbara came in from the office that evening, I was too upset to talk sensibly.

"We're going to lose everything!" I yelled. "We can't make it with all these bills!" I carried on in that vein until I wore myself out, and then I stomped out the door.

After I left the room, Barbara began storming the gates of heaven. "You heard him, Lord. We need money. We've been giving You ten percent of every dollar that comes into this house, and You promised You would supply our needs if we obey Your Word. I know You will!"

Two days later we received a letter in the mail. It was from my doctor at the hospital in Boston. He had written earlier to suggest that I return for a check-up; but I had replied with a note stating that I could walk, was off all medications, and was feeling quite strong again. I had also told him that we were so deeply in debt that I couldn't afford the fifty dollars he charged for each visit.

Now here was his reply. He said, "If you're the way you say you are, come to my office. Not only will I not charge you for the visit, I will waive the four hundred dollars you presently owe me."

Well! God didn't send in the money as Barbara requested. He just cancelled the bill! And, of course, I went to see the doctor.

"Amazing, amazing!" he said as he examined me. I told him God had healed me, but he could only go so far as to give Mother Nature the credit. When I asked him who he thought Mother Nature is, he declined to answer and sent me on my way—debt free! When I recalled that incident, I realized afresh that God would keep His Word and supply everything that was needed for our ministry (Philippians 4:19). All I had to do was trust Him.

Chapter Eleven

THE BLEATING OF SHEEP

I tell you, a shepherd cannot be a proud man. A shepherd must be willing to lay down his life for the sheep,* and humbly care for all their needs. Have I not called you for this purpose, that you might feed My sheep and My lambs? **

When God suggested that I start opening our home for weekly prayer meetings, I confess I didn't like the idea at all.

"Why do that, Lord?" I objected. "I'm an evangelist—remember?"

But God didn't argue with me. He just repeated His

---
* See John 10:11.
** See John 21:15-17.

instructions again and again until I finally gave in, just to get Him off my back.

Prayer meetings! I certainly didn't relish the thought of being saddled with *that* responsibility! I felt like Moses must have felt while tending sheep on the back side of the desert for those forty years before God called him: They weren't even his own sheep; they belonged to his father-in-law. And the people who would come to my home wouldn't "belong" to me either. All of them would have their own churches. I felt that looking after them would be a thankless job, and too much like a pastorate for my blood anyway.

But there was no getting away from what God wanted. He made it clear to me that there were many hungry sheep in the flock who were roaming around in search of food. I had a responsibility to help feed them. So I finally announced a meeting to a few friends, and began.

After several meetings, I began to see that I needed these sheep even more than they needed me. I needed to be reintroduced to people. I had been cooped up by sickness for so long that I had become like a hermit, cut off from the burdens and heartaches of other people. Obviously, if God was ever going to use me in an effective ministry, I'd have to fall in love with people.

First of all, God had to remind me that when people are born again in Christ, they are like baby lambs. They can take only the "milk" of the Word, and they would choke on those "pork chops" I wanted to throw out to them occasionally.

When a "newborn" would express guilt about bothering me with his problems, I'd have to remind him that it was my God-given responsibility to help him. He needed very special attention, just as a lamb does.

Some of them had sicknesses; again and again, they would ask me to pray for them. Some were healed, while others showed no improvement at all. I discovered that in some cases people have a secret sin which allows the devil to keep his foot in the door; until that sin is dealt with, the healing does not come. In actually ministering to people, how much I learned!

I'd have to keep reminding the people who met with us to "come back to basics" and not get off on tangents leading to erroneous doctrines. I'd also remind them to come back to the meetings regularly, become established in the Word, and grow in the Spirit. I'd have to be patient with those who could not understand why a particular cult was false. Sometimes I got to feeling like a parent does with natural children. There are just some things that cannot be explained to a little one. It's like explaining integral calculus to a first-grader. No amount of talking will do any good. The child has to grow up a little before he can come to grips with that. I often realized how Jesus must have felt when He said to His disciples, "I have yet many things to say unto you, but ye cannot bear them now" (John 16:12).

Sometimes I wanted to throw up my hands and quit. But then I'd remember how patient God had been with me when I was so conceited and proud—and my own impatience would put me to shame.

Many times I had to warn them about getting entangled in legalism. Take young Gail Margosian, for instance. She happened to like rather mod clothes and felt comfortable in them. Her choices were never immodest though.

Early in her Christian experience, a certain Christian brother gave her a "word" from the Lord.

"If you don't change your way of dressing," he said, "God will not accept you."

That was bad news for Gail. But I praise the Lord she had sense enough to pray about it. Finally she realized that this man, who grew up in a previous generation, was still hung up on the fashions of those years, and that what really matters to God is the heart of a person—not the clothing.

Although this well-meaning Christian brother did not cause Gail to stumble, yet by his continual expounding on this subject, he *did* cause another babe in Christ to fall away from the faith for a considerable time.

Sometimes a little babe in Christ would become angry at something I said and would leave the safety of the "fold." That was almost like losing a natural child to me, since I knew God had assigned that one to my care.

Then there were those who would run to me when things became a little hot for them in another group where God was dealing with them through someone else. What a challenge it was to help these "runaway sheep"!

I had definitely not wanted to be so deeply involved with people; yet I found myself weeping for them—weeping for their souls, weeping for their sins and sicknesses when they were too shut off from God to weep for themselves, weeping over their trials. I was really beginning to love the Lord's sheep.

Sometimes I'd get a little tickled at them too. I couldn't help but smile at their misdirected enthusiasm—but not wanting to dampen their zeal, I'd just let them experiment with prayer. Quite often I'd hear, "I'm going to pray that God will do such-and-such, or heal So-and-So; if He does, it'll be a great witness to my doctor, or this one or that one."

I wanted them to pray, of course. And sometimes I'd wonder why God didn't seem to care about impressing Doctor So-and-So—but He didn't. So a lot of these prayers never got answered. But each Christian has to learn how to pray in the will of God— and it is the mistakes along the way that help teach us what is right.

One of the most encouraging things was to watch the lambs grow into strong sheep. Some of them— Abbott Bentley, for instance—became good witnesses for Jesus.

"Ben," as we called him, had fallen at the age of seven and injured his left hip. At that time, he had been put into a plaster cast extending from his chest to his knee. After nine months, it was removed and he was able to walk with crutches. Five years later, after much physical therapy, he was finally able to walk without assistance.

When he was around thirty-five years old, he developed severe pains in his leg and went to see his doctor. Ben was told that he had Perthes' disease, which—the doctor explained—is like tuberculosis of the bone. As the disease progresses, the bone degenerates and there is intense pain. It is medically incurable. As a result of the condition, Ben's left leg had shrunk half an inch, causing a slight limp. The doctor advised him to wear a shoe lift, which would push the ball joint up into his hip socket more perfectly and afford some relief.

It was twenty-seven years later—when Ben was sixty-two years old—that I met him. Even though he was a born-again Christian, Ben tells me that he felt a little uncomfortable the first night he came to our prayer meeting. (I could easily understand that when I recalled how uneasy I'd been the night I was saved in the meeting hall over the poolroom.) At our meetings, people always praised God enthusiastically with uplifted hands. After Scripture reading, a little teaching and prayer, I asked if there were special needs. Ben spoke up.

He told us about the half-inch lift in his left shoe. So I asked him to sit down in a chair, and I picked up his feet in my hands so that everyone could see the difference in the length of his legs. When I began to pray, Ben jumped up and grabbed at his left thigh.

"Ouch! Something's happening!" he exclaimed. "I'm being healed!"

Sure enough, when he stood up, both his legs were the same length!

Ben was so excited that he called his doctor the next morning to have X-rays made of his hip. (That was in February, 1972.) When he went in for the X-rays, he took along some films that had been made in 1942, so that the doctor could compare the new ones with the old.

The new X-rays showed Ben's hip to be in better condition than it was thirty years earlier! The doctor said that his left thigh muscle had expanded an inch and a quarter—which explained the pain he had felt in his thigh during the prayer.

Ben told me later, "When I told the doctor that Jesus is curing people today, he said he was a scientist and couldn't believe in divine healing. But he asked to borrow my X-rays to take to a conference!"

Ben learned later that the doctor had shown his colleagues the 1942 X-rays first, and had asked their opinion as to what Ben's condition should be. They all agreed that his hip bone should be deteriorated and that he should be in a wheelchair. Then the doctor brought out Ben's 1972 X-rays. The conclusion these medical men reached was that Ben must be in the "lucky five percent."

"But I know differently!" Ben declared. "The doctor said the pain was gone because 'the fire went out.' It sure did! Praise the Lord—God healed me!"

Not only had Ben's leg been lengthened the night he was prayed for, but an even greater miracle had happened to him. God had healed him of the painful Perthes' disease which had plagued him for fifty-five years. It was testimonies like this that encouraged me to keep pressing on in the ministry.

And then there are Dick and Helen Johnson. When I'm tempted to wonder if I'm wasting my time, I like to get out this letter and read it over:

Dear Barbara and Doug,

Praise the Lord!

The gift Jesus gave to us is priceless, and we will always praise His name. We shall never forget the power of Jesus. . . .

You know; you saw Helen and me. He made us speak in tongues. Helen cried like she has never cried before. . . . She was so thirsty for the Holy Spirit that Jesus filled her to overflowing and made her drunk! I'm sure now that this is a lesson for all of us. When we ask in Jesus' name, He will give to overflowing. . . .

Jesus so filled me that I laughed and laughed more than I have ever laughed before—just from complete joy.

These are the happenings that we shall remember all the days of our lives. When we become low, we will remind one another, and Jesus will lift us up again. Praise the Lord!

                            Dick and Helen Johnson

So it was sheep like Ben, and Dick and Helen Johnson, who gave God the glory, that made the work worthwhile. Little by little, God was showing me that even an evangelist must have a shepherd's heart.

Chapter Twelve

EVERY RUNG GOES HIGHER, HIGHER

When you walked in your own ways, you were as confident as a lion. But when I called you to walk through the valleys of humiliation with Me, you were but a terrified lamb. You drew back and cried out, "Why me?"

But I am the Good Shepherd.* I led you in ways that were needful for you. In every gloomy valley, you learned that I am all you need. No longer are you a weak lamb, but a full-grown sheep, "strong in the Lord," ready for the upward climb.

The more Barbara and I ministered to people, the more we became aware that there were certain ones who had problems that didn't yield to regular treat-

---
* John 10:11.

ment. Though these dear folks prayed and prayed, no victory came. Some of them were sincere Christians who wanted to serve Jesus faithfully—but then some powerful compulsion would come over them, and they'd yield to the very sin they hated.

This wasn't hard for me to understand, though. When I remembered the spirit of depression that had successfully hampered my Christian walk for so long, and how this spirit had to be cast out of me, I realized that some problems can be dealt with in no other way. So I began to teach these people about deliverance from demons. A few of our Christian friends looked down their noses at this kind of ministry and made snide remarks about Barbara and me "getting involved with demons." But I knew in my heart that *casting out* demons is certainly not getting *involved* with them!

I'll never forget the time Valerie's parents, Al and Joan, came to see us, their faces drawn and disconcerted.

"There is definitely something wrong with our Valerie!" Joan said as she sat in our living room. She was quivering all over, tears in her eyes. "Valerie has been seeing a psychiatrist, but she seems to be getting nowhere. Would you see her?"

Al and Joan explained that during the past year Valerie had been experiencing bouts of abnormality when she would scream obscenities at the top of her lungs for apparently no reason at all. These episodes were most embarrassing, especially when they occurred in public places—in shopping areas, restaurants, or even in church.

Immediately Barbara and I recognized what the problem was and said we'd be glad to talk with Valerie if she was willing.

Valerie was a brilliant college student; when we went to see her, she showed real concern for her problem, and openly discussed it.

While talking with her, I sensed the Holy Spirit telling me that the origin of Valerie's troubles was her dabblings in the occult. With that in mind, I questioned her further. She told Barbara and me how her behavior had been perfectly normal until she and a group of her college friends attended a séance. Shortly after that, she said, she began experiencing these alarming bouts of uncontrolled screaming.

"But why did you ever attend such a meeting?" I asked.

"Just because my friends were going," she replied. "Besides, I thought it would be a little innocent fun, and I was game for some excitement."

Valerie's was not a terribly unusual story in our experience. Barbara and I had come across many such people who had become bound by ungodly spirits, not necessarily manifesting themselves in the same way as the one troubling Valerie, but nevertheless binding them. In an evening of innocent experimentation, Valerie had become trapped. Obviously, the screaming and the obscenities were totally inconsistent with the personality of this sweet girl. Now, in desperation and humility, she was pouring her heart out to us.

That day Valerie asked Jesus into her heart. Then, with her cooperation, Barbara and I commanded the foul spirit afflicting her to depart. As we did, the spirit seemed to push her personality aside and yell at us.

"I won't come out! I won't come out!" it said defiantly.

But, nevertheless, it *did* leave as we issued the command in the authority of the name of Jesus. After it came out, Valerie heaved a sigh of relief and sank back into the chair. "I'm free!" she exclaimed, almost in disbelief. "I felt it go!"

We made it very clear to Valerie that she must maintain close fellowship with God if she intended to *remain* free of any further oppression. Demons do not give up easily.

A week later Valerie was baptized in the Holy Spirit. She continued with her psychiatric appointments; but after the second session following her deliverance, the psychiatrist declared her "healed."

Valerie is now leading a happy, guilt-free life. The screaming has not recurred, nor has she had any more interest in the occult. Regular fellowship with Christian people has helped her grow in the faith until she almost glows! She has now graduated from college and is gainfully employed in her chosen profession.

"You know," I commented to Barbara later, "I think I'm beginning to get a little more insight about the dark experiences we've come through. You just can't have much compassion for the problems of other people until you've had a few yourself."

"That's right," Barbara agreed. "It seems as though all of the Lord's sheep go through heartbreak and humiliation. Most of these experiences are far different from Valerie's, but just as real. It's just too bad that there aren't more sympathetic Christians around to reach out a helping hand to the sheep that are troubled."

As Barbara talked, I found my mind wandering off into my own thoughts. I couldn't help thinking about the many Christian friends who had extended their love to me during my troubled days. How could I have ever gotten along without them?

And yet I also knew that the ultimate source of my comfort was Jesus Himself. When I felt confused and crushed by life's circumstances, I understood what Paul meant when he said, "Sometimes I want to live and at other times I don't, for I long to go and be with Christ." * That was the way I felt. I knew the tears would be wiped away when I reached the other side, and I dreamed about that day. But I knew, too, that God was doing something in me down here in these valleys that needed to be done. Obviously, God had a lot of work to do in me before I would be ready for the glory of the other side.

Sometimes, I'd become impatient, and I'd urged the Lord to make me like Jesus more quickly. Then it seemed I could almost hear Him speaking to me like He spoke to James and John, when he said, "Ye know not what ye ask: can ye drink of the cup that I drink of? and be baptized with the baptism that I am baptized with?" **

I also remembered how John the Baptist had said, "He must increase, but I must decrease." † Wasn't

---

* Philippians 1:23, Living Bible.
** Mark 10:38.
† John 3:30.

that the way Jesus had dealt with me? Day after day, He had allowed me to go through humiliations that decreased Doug Foley and forced him to cling to the great hand of God.

Time and again I had been driven to read about Job and how God had allowed his life to be stripped away to practically nothing. But it was through these seemingly unbearable humiliations that Job's self-righteousness was finally exposed and purged. I cried for Job and for myself when I came to understand what God was doing in my life. How sad that God could make me see only by allowing me to be blind—and could make me walk with Him only by allowing me to be crippled with MS.

I recalled hearing about the strange ways of the shepherds of old. If a shepherd had a lamb that continually strayed, he would break one of the lamb's legs so it couldn't walk. Then he would tenderly take that little lamb upon his own shoulders until its leg healed. While that little lamb rested thus on the shepherd, it began to know its master's voice; and when it was recovered, it would stray no more.

Doug Foley was once a crippled lamb—a poor weak thing—until I saw that all the strength I needed was in Jesus—that the weaker I was in myself, the stronger I was becoming in Him—that the farther I went into the dark valleys, the higher I was climbing in the Spirit.

I had discovered that the Christian life is like climbing a ladder. With each new step to a higher rung, I had to cross a certain amount of empty space. Crossing this emptiness represented a little more death to self, a little more crucifixion to selfish desires, before attaining the new height. Just as Jesus accepted crucifixion, He expects His sheep to follow in His footsteps. With me, pride had to be laid on the altar and slain. With you it may be something else. No "crucifixion" has ever been easy. With each, the tears flow, the questions arise, the fears threaten. But just as Jesus endured the cross for the joy that was set before Him,* even so, I came to see that after every trial is joy, and after every crucifixion is fullness of life.

A few days later I said to Barbara, "There have been times when I think I would have been willing to sell my soul to escape from life; but I'm so glad I stuck it out. I've proved God, and He's shown me His love and ability to carry me through. I think I would follow Him anywhere now."

"If that's so," she replied, "then you're on your way up. After all, there isn't any other way to be happy, is there?"

---

* See Hebrews 12:2.

EPILOGUE

My dealings with Doug Foley are not over. I have many more things to teach him, and many ways in which I intend to use him.

When he was strong, his heart was lifted up to his near destruction. But in My mysterious ways, which are higher than man's ways, I brought him down. He who desired to be first became last of all.

I did not deal thus with him because I hated him, but because I loved him enough to save him from himself. I taught him that no man is sufficient unto himself. I taught him that it is from within, out of the heart of man, that pride and evil thoughts proceed.

I made him weak. But let the weak now say, "In Christ, I am strong." For I have chosen the foolish things of the world to confound the wise; and I have chosen the weak things of the world to confound the things which are mighty.

WHEREVER PAPERBACKS ARE SOLD OR USE THIS COUPON

Whitaker House
504 LAUREL DRIVE, MONROEVILLE, PA 15146

SEND INSPIRATIONAL BOOKS LISTED BELOW

Title   Price   ☐ Send Complete Catalog

_____   _____
_____   _____
_____   _____
_____   _____
_____   _____
_____   _____
_____   _____
_____   _____
_____   _____
_____   _____

NAME_____
STREET_____
CITY_____STATE_____ZIP_____

FACE UP WITH A MIRACLE
by Don Basham — $1.25

The Bashams weren't even born again when they went to visit a neighbor in the hospital. She wasn't there. God had healed her! The Bashams had just come *Face Up with a Miracle* —and they were about to come face up with the Holy Spirit . . .

THE PURPLE PIG AND OTHER MIRACLES
by Dick Eastman — $1.45

Hidden away in a rambling, wood frame house on "O" Street in Sacramento, there's a special underground room where Bible-believing Christians pray twenty-four hours a day, seven days a week. Miracles? They happen all the time. And the prayer power is spreading . . .

SCANDALOUS SAINT
by John Hagee — $1.25

The dynamic true story of John and Josie Eils, who were led by the Holy Spirit from one hair-raising scrape into another, only to escape by the skin of their teeth and the grace of God.

THE NEW WINE IS BETTER
by Robert Thom — $1.45

Before the miracle happened, Robert Thom was an alcoholic sailor on the verge of suicide. Afterwards, his life was one miracle after another . . .

SIMMER DOWN, SAINT
by Jody Woerner — $1.25

Anxious? Uptight? Lost your cool? Simmer down—and let the author show you how you can add health, strength, peace, and joy to your Christian experience through the power of the Holy Spirit.

KICKED OUT OF THE KINGDOM
by Charles Trombley
$1.25

Are the days of miracles past? This former Jehovah's Witness thought so, until he became the father of a baby girl with club feet, and he found himself desperately *needing* a miracle . . .

IF I CAN, YOU CAN
by Betty Lee Esses
$2.25

The wife of charismatic teacher Michael Esses tells how Jesus saved her husband and her marriage—and shares what He's been teaching the Esses since.

THE RAPTURE BOOK
by Doug Chatham
$1.25

Some day soon, believers will be caught away and those remaining here on Earth will go through the worst seven years the world will ever know. Ready or not, you owe it to yourself to learn about this next event on the prophetic calendar!

GILLIES' GUIDE TO HOME PRAYER MEETINGS
by George and Harriet Gillies
$1.25

A practical, step-by-step handbook dealing with the problems and procedures involved in setting up the kind of home fellowship that will bless the lives of all attending, written by the authors of *A Scriptural Outline of the Baptism in the Holy Spirit*.

ACTS OF THE GREEN APPLES
by Jean Stone Willans
$1.25

The heart-warming, miracle-studded and hilarious true story of a family of quiet, respectable suburbanites whose lives were turned upside-down by an act of God.